Tales of the Dead

TALES

OF

THE DEAD.

Printed by S. Hamilton, Weybridge.

T·ALES

OF

THE DEAD.

PRINCIPALLY

TRANSLATED FROM THE FRENCH.

Mrs. Utterson

"Graves, at my command,
Have waked their sleepers; oped, and let them forth
By my so potent art."

SHAKSPEARE.

LONDON:

PRINTED FOR WHITE, COCHRANE, AND CO., FLEET-STREET.

1813.

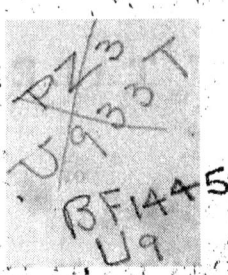

ADVERTISEMENT.

ALTHOUGH the passion for books of amusement founded on the marvellous relative to ghosts and spirits may be considered as having very much subsided; yet I cannot but think that the tales which form the bulk of this little volume, may still afford gratification in the perusal. From the period when the late Lord Orford first published The Castle of Otranto, till the production of Mrs. Ratcliffe's romances, the appetite for the species of reading in question gradually increased; and perhaps it would not have been now surfeited, but for the multitude of contemptible imitations which the popularity of the latter writer called-forth, and which continually issued from the press, until the want of readers at length checked the inundation.

The Northern nations have generally discovered more of imagination in this description of writing than their neighbours in the South or West; and in proportion as they have been more the victims of credulity with respect to spirits, they have indulged in the wanderings of fancy on subjects of this kind, and have eagerly employed their invention in forming narrations founded on the supposed communication between the spiritual world and mankind. The productions of Schiller, and others of the modern German literati, of this nature, are well known in England.

a

The first four tales in this collection, and the last, are imitated from a small French work, which professes to be translated from the German*. It contains several other stories of a similar cast; but which did not appear equally interesting, and they have therefore been omitted. The last tale has been considerably curtailed, as it contained much matter relative to the loves of the hero and heroine, which in a compilation of this kind appeared rather misplaced. The fifth tale, (or rather fragment,) is founded on an incident similar in its features, which was some years since communicated to me, by a female friend of very deserved literary celebrity, as having actually occurred in this country; and I have therefore no other claim in respect to it, than that of having a little amplified the detail.—The termination is abrupt, and necessarily so, as I must candidly confess a want of imagination to fulfil the expectations which may have been excited by the early part of the tale.

The translation was the amusement of an idle hour; and if it afford an equal portion of gratification to the reader, the time has not been altogether misemployed.

* Fantasmagoriana ; ou Recueil d'Histoires d'Apparitions, de Spectres, Revenans, Fantômes, &c. Traduit de l'Allemand, par un Amateur. Paris, 1812. 2 tom. 12mo.

PREFACE

OF

THE FRENCH TRANSLATOR.

———

It is generally believed that at this time of day no one puts any faith in ghosts and apparitions. Yet, on reflection, this opinion does not appear to me quite correct: for, without alluding to workmen in mines, and the inhabitants of mountainous countries,— the former of whom believe in spectres and hobgoblins presiding over concealed treasures, and the latter in apparitions and phantoms announcing either agreeable or unfortunate tidings,—may we not ask why amongst ourselves there are certain individuals who have a dread of passing through a church-yard after night-fall? Why others experience an involuntary shuddering at entering a church, or any other large uninhabited edifice, in the dark? And, in fine, why persons who are deservedly considered as possessing courage and good sense, dare not visit at night even places where they are certain of meeting with nothing they need dread from living beings? They are ever repeating, that the living are only to be dreaded; and yet fear night, because they believe, by tradition, that it is the time which

a 2

phantoms choose for appearing to the inhabitants of
the earth.

Admitting, therefore, as an undoubted fact, that,
with few exceptions, ghosts are no longer believed
in, and that the species of fear we have just mentioned arises from a natural horror of darkness incident to man,—a horror which he cannot account for
rationally,—yet it is well known that he listens with
much pleasure to stories of ghosts, spectres, and
phantoms. The wonderful ever excites a degree of
interest, and gains an attentive ear; consequently,
all recitals relative to supernatural appearances
please us. It was probably from this cause that the
study of the sciences which was in former times in-
termixed with the marvellous; is now reduced to the
simple observation of facts. This wise revolution
will undoubtedly assist the progress of truth; but it
has displeased many men of genius, who maintain that
by so doing, the sciences are robbed of their greatest
attractions, and that the new mode will tend to
weary the mind and disenchant study; and they neglect no means in their power to give back to the supernatural, that empire of which it has been recently
deprived: They loudly applaud their efforts, though
they cannot pride themselves on their success: for
in physic and natural history prodigies are entirely
exploded.

But if in these classes of writing, the marvellous

and supernatural would be improper, at least they cannot be considered as misplaced in the work we are now about to publish : and they cannot have any dangerous tendency on the mind; for the title-page announces extraordinary relations, to which more or less faith may be attached, according to the credulity of the person who reads them. Besides which, it is proper that some repertory should exist, in which we may discover the traces of those superstitions to which mankind have so long been subject. We now laugh at, and turn them into ridicule: and yet it is not clear to me, that recitals respecting phantoms have ceased to amuse; or that, so long as human nature exists, there will be wanting those who will attach faith to histories of ghosts and spectres.

I might in this preface have entered into a learned and methodical disquisition respecting apparitions ; but should only have repeated what Dom Calmet* and the Abbé Lenglet-Dufresnoy† have already said

---

* Dissertation sur les Apparitions, par Dom Augustin Calmet: 3me édition. Paris, 1751, 2 tom. 12mo.

† Traité Historique et Dogmatique sur les Apparitions, les Visions, et les Révélations particuliers; avec des Remarques sur la Dissertation du R. P. Dom Calmet: par l'Abbé Lenglet-Dufresnoy. Avignon ou Paris, 1751. 2 tom. 12mo.

Recueil de Dissertations, Anciennes et Nouvelles, sur les Apparitions, les Visions, et les Songes; avec une Preface historique: par l'Abbé L. Dufresnoy. Avignon ou Paris, 1751. 4 tom. 12mo.

on the subject, and which they have so thoroughly
exhausted, that it would be almost impossible to ad-
vance any thing new. Persons curious to learn every
thing relative to apparitions, will be amply recompensed by consulting the two writers above mentioned.
They give to the full as strange recitals as any which
are to be found in this work. Although the Abbé
Lenglet-Dufresnoy says there really are apparitions;
yet he does not appear to believe in them himself:
but Dom Calmet finishes (as Voltaire observes) as if
he believed what he wrote, and especially with respect
to the extraordinary histories of Vampires. And
we may add, for the benefit of those anxious to make
deeper search into the subject in question, that the
Abbé Lenglet-Dufresnoy has given a list of the principal authors who have written on spirits, demons,
apparitions, dreams, magic, and spectres.

Since this laborious writer has published this list,
Swedenborg and St. Martin have rendered themselves notorious by their Works; and there have also
appeared in Germany treatises on this question of
the appearance of spirits. The two authors who have
the most largely entered into the detail are Wagener
and Jung. The first, whose book is entitled The
Spectres*, endeavours to explain apparitions by at-

* Die Gespenster Kurze Erzæhlungen aus dem Reiche der
Wahrheit. Berlin, 1797, et suiv. in 8vo.

tributing them to natural causes. But the second,
on the contrary, firmly believes in spirits; and his
Theory on Phantasmatology* furnishes us with an
undoubted proof of this assertion. This work, the
fruit of an ardent and exalted imagination, is in some
degree a manual to the doctrines of the modern
Seers, known in Germany under the denomination of
Stillingianer. They take their name from *Stilling*,
under which head Jung has written memoirs of his
life, which forms a series of different works. This
sect, which is actually in existence, is grafted on the
Swedenborgians and Martinismc, and has a great
number of adherents, especially in Switzerland. We
also see in the number of the (*English*) Monthly
Review for December 1811, that Mrs. Grant has
given a pretty circumstantial detail of the apparitions and spirits to which the Scottish mountaineers
attach implicit faith.

In making choice of the stories for my translations
from the German, which I now offer to the public,
I have neglected nothing to merit the approbation of
those who take pleasure in this species of reading:
and if this selection has the good fortune to meet
with any success, it shall be followed by another; in
which I shall equally endeavour to excite the curiosity of the lovers of romance; while to those who are

* Theorie der Geister-Kunde. Nuremberg, 1808, in 8vo.—This
work has been censured by several Protestant consistories.

difficult to please, and to whom it seems strange that
any one should attach the slightest degree of faith to
such relations, I merely say,—Remember the words
of Voltaire, at the beginning of the article he wrote
on " *Apparition,*" in his Philosophical Dictionary:
"*It is no uncommon thing for a person of lively feelings to fancy he sees what never really existed.*"

TALES

OF

THE DEAD.

TALES OF THE DEAD.

I.

THE FAMILY PORTRAITS.

" No longer shall you gaze on't; lest your fancy
May think anon, it moves.————
The fixure of her eye has motion in't."

WINTER'S TALE.

NIGHT had insensibly superseded day, when Ferdinand's carriage continued its slow course through the forest; the postilion uttering a thousand complaints on the badness of the roads, and Ferdinand employing the leisure which the tedious progress of his carriage allowed, with reflections to which the purpose of his journey gave rise.

. As was usual with young men of rank, he had visited several universities; and after having travelled over the principal parts of Europe, he was now returning to his native country to take possession of the property of his father, who had died in his absence.

Ferdinand was an only son, and the last branch of the ancient family of Meltheim: it was on this account that his mother was the more anxious that

he should form a brilliant alliance, to which both his
birth and fortune entitled him; she frequently repeated that Clotilde of Hainthal was of all others
the person she should be most rejoiced to have as
a daughter-in-law, and who should give to the
world an heir to the name and estates of Meltheim. In the first instance, she merely named
her amongst other distinguished females whom
she recommended to her son's attention: but
after a short period she spoke of none but her:
and at length declared, rather positively, that all
her happiness depended on the completion of this
alliance, and hoped her son would approve her
choice.

Ferdinand, however, never thought of this union
but with regret; and the urgent remonstrances
which his mother ceased not to make on the subject, only contributed to render Clotilde, who was
an entire stranger to him, less amiable in his eyes:
he determined at last to take a journey to the ca-
-pital, whither Mr. Hainthal and his daughter
were attracted by the carnival. He wished at
least to know the lady, ere he consented to listen
to his mother's entreaties; and secretly flattered
himself that he should find some more cogent
reasons for opposing this union than mere caprice,
which was the appellation the old lady gave to his
repugnance.

: Whilst travelling alone in his carriage, as night.
approached, the solitary forest, his imagination
drew a picture of his early life, which happy re-
collections rendered still happier. It seemed, that
the future presented no charms for him to equal
the past; and the greater pleasure he took in re-
tracing what no longer existed, the less wish he
felt to bestow a thought on that futurity to which,
contrary to his inclinations, he seemed destined.
Thus, notwithstanding the slowness with which his
carriage proceeded over the rugged ground, he
found that he was too rapidly approaching the
termination of his journey. . . . .

The postilion at length began to console himself; for one half of the journey was accomplished,
and the remainder presented only good roads: Ferdinand, however, gave orders to his groom to stop
at the approaching village, determining to pass the
night there. . . . .

The road through the village which led to the
inn was bordered by gardens, and the sound of
different musical instruments led Ferdinand to
suppose that the villagers were celebrating some
rural *fête*. He already anticipated the pleasure
of joining them, and hoped that this recreation
would dissipate his melancholy thoughts. But on
listening more attentively, he remarked that the
music did not resemble that usually heard at inns;

and the great light he perceived at the window of
a pretty house from whence came the sounds that
had arrested his attention, did not permit him to
doubt that a more select party than are accustomed to reside in the country at that unfavourable
season, were amusing themselves in performing a
concert.

The carriage now stopped at the door of a
small inn of mean appearance. Ferdinand, who
counted on much inconvenience and few comforts,
asked who was the lord of the village. They informed him that he occupied a *château* situated
in an adjoining hamlet. Our traveller said no more,
but was obliged to content himself with the best
apartment the landlord could give him. To divert
his thoughts, he determined to walk in the village,
and directed his steps towards the spot where he
had heard the music; to this the harmonious
sounds readily guided him: he approached softly,
and found himself close to the house where the
concert was performing. A young girl, sitting at
the door, was playing with a little dog, who began
to bark. Ferdinand, drawn from his reverie by
this singular accompaniment, begged the little girl
to inform him who lived in that house. "It is
my father," she replied, smiling; "come in, sir."
And saying this, she slowly went up the steps.

Ferdinand hesitated for an instant whether to

accept this unceremonious invitation. But the
master of the house came down, saying to him in
a friendly tone : " Our music, sir, has probably
been the only attraction to this spot; no matter, it
is the pastor's, abode, and to it you are heartily
welcome. My neighbours and I," continued he,
whilst leading Ferdinand, in, " meet alternately
at each other's houses once a week, to form
a little concert; and to-day it is my turn. Will
you take a part in the performance, or only listen
to it? Sit down in this apartment. Are you accustomed to hear better music than that performed
simply by amateurs? or do you prefer an assemblage
where they pass their time in conversation? If you
like the latter, go into the adjoining room, where
you will find my wife surrounded by a young circle;
here is our musical party, there is their *conver-
sazióni.*" Saying this, he opened the door, made
a gentle inclination of the head to Ferdinand, and
seated himself before his desk. Our traveller
would fain have made apologies; but the performers in an instant resumed the piece he had
interrupted. At the same time the pastor's wife,
a young and pretty woman, entreated Ferdinand,
in the most gracious manner possible, entirely to
follow his own inclinations, whether they led him
to remain with the musicians, or to join the circle
assembled in the other apartment. Ferdinand,

after uttering some common-place terms of politeness, followed her into the adjoining room. . .

The chairs formed a semicircle round the sofa,
and were occupied by several women and by some
men. They all rose on Ferdinand's entering, and
appeared a little disconcerted at the interruption.
In the middle of the circle was a low chair, on
which sat, with her back to the door, a young and
sprightly female, who, seeing every one rise,
changed her position, and at sight of a stranger
blushed and appeared embarrassed. Ferdinand
entreated the company not to interrupt the conversation. They accordingly reseated themselves,
and the mistress of the house invited the new guest
to take a seat on the sofa by two elderly ladies,
and drew her chair near him. " The music," she
said to him, " drew you amongst us, and yet in
this apartment we have none; I hear it nevertheless
with pleasure myself: but I cannot participate in
my husband's enthusiasm for simple quartetts and
symphonies; several of my friends are of the same
way of thinking with me, which is the reason that,
while our husbands are occupied with their favourite science, we here enjoy social converse, which
sometimes, however, becomes too loud for our
virtuoso neighbours. To-day, I give a long-pro-
mised tea-drinking. Every one is to relate a story
of ghosts, or something of a similar nature. You

see that my auditors are more numerous than the band of musicians."

" Permit me, madam," replied Ferdinand, " to add to the number of your auditors; although I have not much talent in explaining the marvellous."

" That will not be any hinderance to you here," answered a very pretty brunette; " for it is agreed amongst us that no one shall search for any expla- nation, even though it bears the stamp of truth, as explanations would take away all pleasure from ghost stories."

" I shall benefit by your instructions," answered Ferdinand: " but without doubt I interrupt a very interesting recital;—dare I entreat—?"

The young lady with flaxen hair, who rose from the little seat, blushed anew; but the mistress of the house drew her by the arm, and laughing, con- ducted her to the middle of the circle. " Come, child," said she, " don't make any grimace; reseat yourself, and relate your story. This gentleman will also give us his."

" Do you promise to give us one, sir?" said the young lady to Ferdinand. He replied by a low bow. She then reseated herself in the place des- tined for the narrator, and thus began:

" One of my youthful friends, named Juliana, passed every summer with her family at her father's estate. The *château* was situated in a romantic

country; high mountains formed a circle in the distance; forests of oaks and fine groves surrounded
it. It was an ancient edifice, and had descended.
through a long line of ancestry to Juliana's father;
for which reason, instead of making any alterations,
he was only anxious to preserve it in the same state
they had left it to him. .   :

"Among the number of antiquities most prized
by him was the family picture gallery; a vaulted
room, dark, high, and of gothic architecture, where
hung the portraits of his forefathers, as large as the
natural size, covering the walls, which were black-
ened by age. Conformable to an immemorial
custom, they ate in this room: and Juliana has
often told me, that she could not overcome, especially at supper-time, a degree of fear and repugnance; and that she had frequently feigned indisposition, to avoid entering this formidable apartment. Among the portraits there was one of a
female, who, it would seem, did not belong to the
family; for Juliana's father could neither tell whom
it represented, nor how it had become ranged
amongst his ancestry: but as to all appearance it
had retained its station for ages, my friend's father
was unwilling to remove it.   . .

" Juliana never looked at this portrait without
an involuntary shuddering: and she has told me,
that from her earliest infancy she has felt this

secret terror, without being able to define the
cause. Her father treated this sentiment as pue-
rile, and compelled her sometimes to remain alone
in that room. But as Juliana grew up, the terror
this singular portrait occasioned, increased; and she
frequently supplicated her father, with tears in her
eyes, not to leave her alone in that apartment—
'That portrait,' she would say, ' regards me not
gloomily or terribly, but with looks full of a mild
melancholy.' It appears anxious to draw me to it,
and as if the lips were about to open and speak to
me.—That picture will certainly cause my death.'

" Juliana's father at length relinquished all hope
of conquering his daughter's fears. One night at
supper, the terror she felt had thrown her into
convulsions, for she fancied she saw the picture
move its lips; and the physician enjoined her father
in future to remove from her view all similar causes
of fear. In consequence, the terrifying portrait
was removed from the gallery, and it was placed
over the door of an uninhabited room in the attic
story.

" Juliana, after this removal, passed two years
without experiencing any alarms. Her com-
plexion resumed its brilliancy, which surprised
every one; for her continual fears had rendered
her pale and wan: but the portrait and the fears it
produced had alike disappeared, and Juliana —"

"Well," cried the mistress of the house, smiling,
when she perceived that the narrator appeared to
hesitate, "confess it, my dear child ; Juliana found
an admirer of her beauty ;—was it not so ?".
. "'Tis even so," resumed the young lady, blushing deeply ;. "she was affianced : and her intended
husband coming to see her the day previous to
that fixed on for her marriage, she, conducted him
over the *château*, and from the attic rooms was
shewing him the. beautiful prospect. which extended to the distant mountains. On a sudden
she found herself, without being aware of it, in
the room where the unfortunate portrait. was
placed. And it was natural that a stranger, surprised at seeing it there alone, should ask who it
represented. To look at it, recognise it, utter a
piercing shriek, and run towards the door, were but
the work of an instant with poor Juliana. But
whether in effect owing to the violence with which
she opened the door the picture was shaken, or
whether the moment was arrived in which its
baneful influence was to be exercised over Juliana,
I know not ; but at the moment this unfortunate
girl was striving to get out of the room and avoid
her destiny, the portrait fell ; and Juliana, thrown
down by her fears, and overpowered by the heavy
weight of the picture, never rose more."——
A long silence followed this recital, which was

only interrupted by the exclamations of surprise and interest excited for the unfortunate Juliana; Ferdinand alone appeared untouched by the general emotions. At length, one of the ladies sitting near him broke the silence by saying, "This story is literally true; I knew the family where the fatal portrait caused the death of a charming young girl: I have also seen the picture; it has, as the young lady truly observed, an indescribable air of goodness which penetrates the heart; so that I could not bear to look on it long; and yet, as you say, its look is so full of tender melancholy, and has such infinite attractions, that it appears that the eyes move and have life."

"In general," resumed the mistress of the house, at the same time shuddering, "I don't like portraits, and I would not have any in the rooms I occupy. They say that they become pale when the original expires; and the more faithful the likeness, the more they remind me of those waxen figures I cannot look at without aversion."

"That is the reason," replied the young person who had related the history, "that I prefer those portraits where the individual is represented occupied in some employment, as then the figure is entirely independent of those who look at it; whereas in a simple portrait the eyes are inanimately fixed on every thing that passes. Such portraits

appear to me as contrary to the laws of illusion as
painted statues."

"I participate in your opinion," replied Ferdinand; "for the remembrance of a terrible impression produced on my mind when young, by a
portrait of that sort, will never be effaced."

"O! pray relate it to us," said the young lady
with flaxen hair, who had not as yet quitted the
low chair; "you are obliged according to promise
to take my place." She instantly arose, and jokingly
forced Ferdinand to change seats with her.

"This history," said he, "will resemble a little
too much the one you have just related; permit me
therefore ——"

"That does not signify," resumed the mistress
of the house, "one is never weary with recitals
of this kind; and the greater repugnance I feel in
looking at these horrible portraits, the greater is
the pleasure I take in listening to histories of their
eyes or feet being seen to move."

"But seriously," replied Ferdinand, who would
fain have retracted his promise, "my history is too
horrible for so fine an evening. I confess to you
that I cannot think of it without shuddering, although several years have elapsed since it happened."

"So much the better, so much the better!"
cried nearly all present; "how you excite our

curiosity! and its having happened to yourself will·
afford double pleasure, as we cannot entertain any,
doubt of the fact."

" It did not happen personally to me," answered·
Ferdinand, who reflected that he had gone too·
far, " but to one of my friends, on whose word I·
have as firm a reliance as if I had been myself a
witness to it."

They reiterated their entreaties ; and Ferdinand
began in these words :—" One day, when I was
arguing with the friend of whom I am about to
make mention, on apparitions and omens, he told
me the following story :—

" I had been invited,' said he, ' by one of my
college companions, to pass my vacations with
him at an estate of his father's. The spring was
that year unusually late, owing to a long and severe
winter, and appeared in consequence more gay
and agreeable, which gave additional charms to
our projected pleasures. We arrived at his father's
in the pleasant mouth of April, animated by all the
gaiety the season inspired.

" As my companion and I were accustomed to
live together at the university, he had recommended
to his family, in his letters, so to arrange matters
that we might live together at his father's also: we
in consequence occupied two adjoining rooms,
from whence we enjoyed a view of the garden and·

a fine country, bounded in the distance by forests
and vineyards. In a few days I found myself so
completely at home in the house, and so famili-.
arised with its inhabitants, that nobody, whether of
the family or among the domesticks, made any difference between my friend and myself. His younger
brothers, who were absent from me in the day,
often passed the night in my room, or in that of
their elder brother. Their sister, a charming girl
about twelve years of age, lovely and blooming as
a newly blown rose, gave me the appellation of
brother, and fancied that under this title she was
privileged to shew me all her favourite haunts in
the garden, to gratify my wishes at table, and to
furnish my apartment with all that was requisite.
Her cares and attention will never be effaced from
my recollection; they will long outlive the scenes
of horror that *château* never ceases to recall to
my recollection. From the first of my arrival, I
had remarked a huge portrait affixed to the wall of
an antechamber through which I was obliged to
pass to go to my room; but, too much occupied
by the new objects which on all sides attracted
my attention, I had not particularly examined it.
Meanwhile I could not avoid observing that,
though the two younger brothers of my friend
were so much attached to me, that they would
never permit me to go at night into my room

without them, yet they always evinced an unac-
countable dread in crossing the hall where this
picture hung. They clung to me, and embraced
me that I might take them in my arms; and
whichever I was compelled to take by the hand,
invariably covered his face, in order that he might
not see the least trace of the portrait.

"Being aware that the generality of children
are afraid of colossal figures, or even of those of
a natural height, I endeavoured to give my two
young friends courage. However, on more attentively considering the portrait which caused them
so much dread, I could not avoid feeling a degree
of fear myself. The picture represented a knight
in the costume of a very remote period; a full grey
mantle descended from his shoulders to his knees;
one of his feet placed in the foreground, appeared
as if it was starting from the canvass; his countenance had an expression which petrified me with
fear. I had never before seen any thing at all
like it in nature. It was a frightful mixture of the
stillness of death, with the remains of a violent
and baneful passion, which not even death itself
was able to overcome. One would have thought
the artist had copied the terrible features of one
risen from the grave, in order to paint this terrific
portrait. I was seized with a terror little less
than the children, whenever I wished to con-

template this picture. Its aspect was disagreeable
to my friend, but did not cause him any terror:
his sister was the only one who could look at this
hideous figure with a smiling countenance; and
said to me with a compassionate air, when I discovered my aversion to it, 'That man is not wicked,
but he is certainly very unhappy.' My friend told
me that the picture represented the founder of his
race, and that his father attached uncommon value
to it; it had, in all probability, hung there from
time immemorial, and it would not be possible to
remove it from this chamber without destroying the
regularity of its appearance.

"Meanwhile, the term of our vacation was
speedily drawing to its close, and time insensibly
wore away in the pleasures of the country. The
old count, who remarked our reluctance to quit
him, his amiable family, his *château*, and the
fine country that surrounded it, applied himself
with kind and unremitting care, to make the day
preceding our departure a continual succession of
rustic diversions: each succeeded the other without
the slightest appearance of art; they seemed of
necessity to follow each other. The delight that
illumined the eyes of my friend's sister when she
perceived her father's satisfaction; the joy that
was painted in Emily's countenance (which was
the name of this charming girl) when she surprised

even her father by her arrangements, which out-
stripped his projects, led me to discover the entire
confidence that existed between the father and
daughter, and the active part Emily had taken in
directing the order which reigned in that day's
festivities. .., ..., ...
.. " Night arrived ; the company in the gardens
dispersed ; but my amiable companions never
quitted my side. The two young boys skipped
gaily before us, chasing the may-bug, and shaking
the shrubs to make them come out. The dew
arose, and aided by the light of the moon formed
silver spangles on the flowers and grass. Emily hung
on my arm ; and an affectionate sister conducted
me, as if to take leave, to all the groves and places
I had been accustomed to visit with her, or with
the family. On arriving at the door of the *château*,
I was obliged to repeat the promise I had made to
her father, of passing some weeks in the autumn
with him. 'That season,' said she, ' is equally beautiful with the spring !... With what pleasure did I
promise to decline all other engagements for this.
Emily retired to her apartment, and, according to
custom, I went up to mine, accompanied by my
two little boys: they ran gaily up the stairs; and
in crossing the range of apartments but faintly
lighted, to my no small surprise their boisterous
mirth was not interrupted by the terrible portrait.

" For my own part, my head and heart were
full of the intended journey, and of the agreeable
manner in which my time had passed at the count's
château. The images of those happy days crowded
on my recollection; my imagination, at that time
possessing all the vivacity of youth, was so much
agitated, that I could not enjoy the sleep which
already overpowered my friend. Emily's image,
so interesting by her sprightly grace, by her pure
affection for me, was present to my mind like an
amiable phantom shining in beauty. I placed
myself at the window, to take another look at
the country I had so frequently ranged with her,
and traced our steps again probably for the last
time. I remembered each spot illumined by the
pale light the moon afforded. The nightingale
was singing in the groves where we had delighted
to repose ; the little river on which while gaily
singing we often sailed, rolled murmuringly her
silver waves.

"Absorbed in a profound reverie, I mentally
exclaimed : With the flowers of spring, this soft
pure peaceful affection will probably fade ; and as
frequently the after seasons blight the blossoms
and destroy the promised fruit, so possibly may
the approaching autumn envelop in cold reserve
that heart which, at the present moment, appears
only to expand with mine !

" Saddened by these reflections, I withdrew
from the window, and overcome by a painful
agitation I traversed the adjoining rooms ; and
on a sudden found myself before the portrait of
my friend's ancestor. The moon's beams darted
on it in the most singular manner possible, in-
somuch as to give the appearance of a horrible
moving spectre; and the reflexion of the light
gave to it the appearance of a real substance about
to quit the darkness by which it was, surrounded.
The inanimation of its features appeared to give
place to the most profound melancholy; the sad
and glazed look of the eyes appeared the only
hinderance to its uttering its grief.
" My knees tremblingly knocked against each
other, and with an unsteady step I regained, my
chamber : the window still remained open; I
reseated myself at it; in order that the freshness of
the night air, and the aspect of the beautiful sur-
rounding country, might dissipate the terror I had
experienced. My wandering eyes fixed on a long
vista of ancient linden trees, which extended from
my window to the ruins of an old tower, which
had often been the scene of our pleasures and
rural fêtes. The remembrance of the hideous
portrait had vanished ; when on a sudden there
appeared to me a thick fog issuing from the ruined

tower, which advancing through the vista of lin-
dens came towards me. ' ; , ./ ' ; . !; ;· ·ƒ.
[. " I regarded this cloud with an anxious curiosity:
it approached; but again it was concealed by the
thickly-spreading branches of the trees. ' ' : ·'
-. "On a sudden I perceived, in a spot of the
avenue 'less dark than the rest, the same figure
represented in the formidable picture, enveloped
in the grey mantle I so well knew. It advanced
towards the *château*, as if hesitating: no noise was
heard of its footsteps on the pavement; it passed
before my window without looking up, and gained
a back door which led to the apartments in the
colonnade of the *château*. ·: ·.: ·' ·' ·
:. " Seized with trembling apprehension, I darted
towards my bed, and saw with pleasure that the
two children were fast asleep on either side.' The
noise I made awoke them; they started, but in an
instant were asleep again. · The agitation I had
endured took from me the power of sleep, and I
turned to awake one of the children to talk with
me: but no powers can depict the horrors I endured when I saw the frightful figure at the side of
the child's bed. ' ·' ' · · · ·;. ! (·. ·
:· " I was petrified with horror, and dared neither
move nor shut my eyes. I beheld the spectre stoop
towards the child and softly kiss his forehead: he

then went round the bed, and kissed the forehead
of the other boy.

"I lost all recollection at that moment; and
the following morning, when the children awoke
me with their caresses, I was willing to consider
the whole as a dream.

"Meanwhile, the moment for our departure was
at hand. We once again breakfasted all together
in a grove of lilacs and flowers. 'I advise you to
take a little more care of yourself,' said the old
count in the midst of other conversation; 'for I last
night saw you walking rather late in the garden, in a
dress ill suited to the damp air; and I was fearful
such imprudence would expose you to cold and
fever. Young people are apt to fancy they are
invulnerable; but I repeat to you, Take advice
from a friend.'

"'In truth,' I answered, 'I believe readily that
I have been attacked by a violent fever, for never
before was I so harassed by terrifying visions : I can
now conceive how dreams afford to a heated imagination subjects for the most extraordinary stories
of apparitions.'

"'What would you tell me?' demanded the
count in a manner not wholly devoid of agitation.
I related to him all that I had seen the preceding
night; and to my great surprise he appeared to me
in no way astonished, but extremely affected.

" ' You say,' added he in a trembling voice,
' that the phantom kissed the two children's fore-
heads?'. I answered him, that it, was even so.
He then exclaimed, in accents of the deepest despair, ' Oh heavens! they must then both die!' "—

Till now the company had listened without the
slightest noise or interruption to Ferdinand: but as
he pronounced the last words, the greater part of
his audience trembled; and the young lady who had
previously occupied the chair on which he sat,
uttered a piercing shriek.

" Imagine," continued Ferdinand, " how astonished my friend must have been at this unexpected exclamation. The vision of the night had
caused him excess of agitation; but the melancholy
voice of the count pierced his heart, and seemed
to annihilate his being, by the terrifying conviction
of the existence of the spiritual world, and the secret horrors with which this idea was accompanied.
It was not then a dream, a chimera, the fruit of an
over-heated imagination! but a mysterious and
infallible messenger, which, dispatched from the
world of spirits, had passed close to him, had
placed itself by his couch, and by its fatal kiss had
dropt the germ of death in the bosom of the two
children.

" He vainly entreated the count to explain this
extraordinary event. Equally fruitless were his son's

endeavours to obtain from the count the develope-
ment of this mystery, which apparently concerned
the whole family. ' You are as yet, too young,'
replied the count: ' too soon, alas! for your peace
of mind, will you be informed of these terrible circumstances which you now think mysterious.' '

" Just as they came to announce to my friend
that all was ready, he recollected that during the
recital the count had sent away Emily and her two
younger brothers. Deeply agitated, he took leave
of the count and the two young children who came
towards him, and who would scarcely permit
themselves to be separated from him. Emily, who
had placed herself at a window, made a sign of
adieu. Three days afterwards the young count
received news of the death of his two younger
brothers. They were both taken off in the same
night.

" You see," continued Ferdinand, in a gayer
tone, in order to counteract the impression of sadness and melancholy his story had produced on the
company; " You see my history is very far from
affording any natural explication of the wonders
it contains; explanations which only tend to shock
one's reason: it does not even make you entirely
acquainted with the mysterious person, which one
has a right to expect in all marvellous recitals.
But I could learn nothing more; and the old count

dying without· revealing, the mystery to his son,· I
see no other means of terminating the history of
the portrait,· which is undoubtedly by no 'means
devoid of interest', than by inventing according to
one's fancy a *dénouement* which shall explain all."
  "That does not appear.at all necessary to me,"
said a young man: " this history, like the one that
preceded it, is in reality finished, and gives all the
satisfaction: one has any right to expect from recitals of this species.".
  "I should not agree with you," replied Ferdinand, " if I was capable of explaining the mysterious connection between the portrait and the death
of the two children in the same night, or the terror
of Juliana at sight of the other portrait, and
her death, consequently caused by it. I am, however, not the less obliged to you for the entire
satisfaction you evince."
  " But," resumed the young man, " what benefit
would your imagination receive, if the connections
of which you speak were known to you?"
  " Very great benefit, without doubt," replied
Ferdinand; " for imagination requires the completion of the objects it represents, as much as the
judgment requires correctness and accuracy in its
ideas!".
  The mistress of the house, not being partial to
these metaphysical disputes, took part with Fer-

dinand: "We ladies," said she, " are always curious; therefore don't wonder that we complain when a story has no termination. It appears to me like seeing the last scene of Mozart's Don Juan without having witnessed the preceding ones; and I am sure no one would be the better satisfied, although the last scene should possess infinite merit."

The young man remained silent, perhaps less through conviction than politeness. Several persons were preparing to retire, and Ferdinand, who had vainly searched with all his eyes for the young lady, with flaxen hair, was already at the door; when an elderly gentleman, whom he remembered to have seen in the music-room, asked him whether the friend concerning whom he had related the story was not called Count Meltheim?

"That is his name," answered Ferdinand a little drily ; "how did you guess it?—are you acquainted with his family?"

"You have advanced nothing but the simple truth," resumed the unknown. "Where is the count at this moment?"

"He is on his travels," replied Ferdinand. "But I am astonished——"

"Do you correspond with him?" demanded the unknown.

"I do," answered Ferdinand.. "But I don't understand——"

"Well then," continued the old man, "tell him
that Emily still continues to think of him, and that
he must return as speedily as possible, if he takes
any interest in a secret that very particularly concerns her family."

On this the old man stepped into his carriage,
and had vanished from Ferdinand's sight ere he
had recovered from his surprise. He looked
around him in vain for some one who might inform him of the name of the unknown: every one
was gone; and he was on the point of risking being
considered indiscreet, by asking for information of
the pastor who had so courteously treated him,
when they fastened the door of the house, and he
was compelled to return in sadness to his inn, and
leave his researches till the morning.

The frightful scenes of the night preceding Ferdinand's departure from the *château* of his friend's
father, had tended to weaken the remembrance of
Emily; and the distraction which his journey so
immediately after had produced, had not contributed to recall it with any force: but all at once
the recollection of Emily darted across his mind
with fresh vigour, aided by the recital of the previous evening and the old man's conversation: it

presented itself even with greater vivacity and
strength than at the period of its birth. Ferdinand
now fancied that he could trace Emily in the pretty
girl with flaxen hair. The more he reflected on
her figure, her eyes, the sound of her voice, the
grace with which she moved; the more striking
the resemblance appeared to him. The piercing
shriek that had escaped her, when he mentioned
the old count's explication of the phantom's appearance; her sudden disappearance at the termination of the recital; her connection with Ferdinand's family, (for the young lady, in her history
of Juliana, had recounted the fatal accident which
actually befel Ferdinand's sister,) all gave a degree
of certainty to his suppositions.

He passed the night in forming projects and
plans, in resolving doubts and difficulties; and Ferdinand impatiently waited for the day which was
to enlighten him. He went to the pastor's, whom
he found in the midst of his quires of music; and
by giving a natural turn to the conversation, he
seized the opportunity of enquiring concerning the
persons with whom he had passed the preceding
evening.

He unfortunately, however, could not get satisfactory answers to his questions concerning the
young lady with flaxen hair, and the mysterious old
gentleman; for the pastor had been so absorbed in

his music, that he had not paid attention to many,
persons who had visited him : and though Ferdinand in the most minute manner possible described
their dress and other particulars, it was impossible
to make the pastor comprehend the individuals
whose names he was so anxious to learn. "It is
unfortunate," said the pastor, "that my wife should
be out; she would have given you all the information you desire. But according to your description, it strikes me the young person with flaxen
hair must be Mademoiselle de Hainthal;—but—"

"Mademoiselle de Hainthal!" reiterated Ferdinand, somewhat abruptly.

"I think so," replied the clergyman. "Are you
acquainted with the young lady ?"

"I know her family," answered Ferdinand;
"but from her features bearing so strong a resemblance to the family, I thought it might have been
the young countess of Wartbourg, who was so
much like her brother."

"That is very possible," said the pastor. "You
knew then the unfortunate count Wartbourg ?"

"Unfortunate !" exclaimed Ferdinand; greatly
surprised.

"You don't then know any thing," continued
the pastor, "of the deplorable event that has recently taken place at the *château* of Wartbourg ?
The young count, who had probably in his travels

seen some beautifully laid-out gardens, was anxious
to embellish the lovely country which surrounds
his *château*; and as the ruins of an old tower
seemed to be an obstacle to his plans, he ordered
them to be pulled down.... His gardener, in vain
represented to him, that seen from one of the wings
of the *château* they presented, at the termination
of a majestic and ancient avenue of linden trees, a
magnificent *coup d'œil*, and that they would also
give a more romantic appearance to the new parts
they were about to form. An old servant, grown
grey in the service of his forefathers, supplicated
him with tears in his eyes to spare the venerable
remains of past ages. They even told him of an
ancient tradition, preserved in the neighbourhood,
which declared, that the existence of the house of
Wartbourg was by supernatural means linked with
the preservation of that tower.

"The count, who was a well-informed man, paid
no attention to these sayings; indeed they possibly
made him the more firmly adhere to his resolution.
The workmen were put to their task: the walls,
which were constructed of huge masses of rock,
for a long while resisted the united efforts of tools
and gunpowder; the architect of this place appeared to have built it for eternity.

"At length perseverance and labour brought it
down. A piece of the rock separating from the

rest, precipitated itself into an opening which had been concealed for ages by rubbish and loose sticks, and fell into a deep cavern. An immense subterranean vault was discovered by the rays of the setting sun, supported by enormous pillars :— but ere they proceeded in their researches, they went to inform the young count of the discovery they had made.

" He came; and being curious to see this dark abode, descended into it with two servants. The first thing they discovered were chains covered with rust, which being fixed in the rock, plainly shewed the use formerly made of the cavern. On another side was a corpse, dressed in female attire of centuries past, which had surprisingly resisted the ravages of time : close to it was extended a human skeleton almost destroyed.

" The two servants related that the young count, on seeing the body, cried in an accent of extreme horror, ' Great God ! it is she then whose portrait killed my intended wife.' Saying which, he fell senseless by the body. The shake which his fall occasioned reduced the skeleton to dust.

" They bore the count to his *château*, where the care of the physicians restored him to life; but he did not recover his senses. It is probable that this tragical event was caused by the confined and unwholesome air of the cavern. A

very few days after, the count died in a state of
total derangement.

" It is singular enough, that the termination of his
life should coincide with the destruction of the ruined tower, and there no longer exists any male branch
of that family. The deeds relative to the succession, ratified and sealed by the emperor Otho, are
still amongst the archives of his house. Their contents have as yet only been transmitted verbally
from father to son, as an hereditary secret, which
will now, however, be made known. It is also
true, that the affianced bride of the count was
killed by the portrait's falling on her."

" I yesterday heard that fatal history recited by
the lady with flaxen hair," replied Ferdinand.

" It is very possible that young person is the
countess Emily," replied the pastor ; " for she was
the bosom-friend of the unfortunate bride."

" Does not then the countess Emily live at the
castle of Wartbourg ?" asked Ferdinand.

"Since her brother's death," answered the clergyman, " she has lived with a relation of her
mother's at the *château* of Libinfelt, a short
distance from hence. For as they yet know not
with certainty to whom the castle of Wartbourg
will belong, she prudently lives retired."

Ferdinand had learnt sufficient to make him
abandon the projected journey to the capital. He

D

thanked the pastor, for, the instructions he had
given him, and was conducted to the *château*
where Emily now resided. ⎜⠄⠄⠄⠄⠄⠄⠄⠄⠄⠄⠄⠄⠄⠄
- It was still broad day when he arrived.⎜ The
whole journey he was thinking of the amiable figure
which he had recognised too late the preceding
evening. He recalled to his idea her every word, the
sound of her voice, her actions; and what his memory failed to represent, his imagination depicted
with all the vivacity of youth, and all the fire of re-
kindled affection. He already addressed secret reproaches to Emily for not recognising him; as if
he had himself remembered her; and in order to
ascertain whether his features were entirely effaced
from the recollection of her whom he adored, he
caused himself to be announced as a stranger, who
was anxious to see her on family matters.

While waiting impatiently in the room into
which they had conducted him, he discovered
among the portraits with which it was decorated,
that of the young lady whose features had the
over-night charmed him anew: he was contemplating it with rapture when the door opened and
Emily entered. She instantly recognised Ferdinand; and in the sweetest accents accosted him as
the friend of her youth.

Surprise rendered Ferdinand incapable of an-
swering suitably to so gracious a reception: it was

not the charming person with flaxen hair; it was
not a figure corresponding with his imagination,
which at this moment presented itself to his view.
But it was Emily, shining in every possible beauty,
far beyond what Ferdinand had expected: he recollected notwithstanding each feature which had
already charmed him, but now clothed in every
perfection which nature bestows on her most favoured objects. Ferdinand was lost in thought
for some moments: he dared not make mention of
his love, and still less did he dare speak of the portrait, and the other wonders of the castle of Wartbourg. Emily spoke only of the happiness she
had experienced in her earlier days, and slightly
mentioned her brother's death.

As the evening advanced, the young female with
flaxen hair came in with the old stranger. Emily
presented them both to Ferdinand, as the baron of
Hainthal and his daughter Clotilde. They remembered instantly the stranger whom they had seen
the preceding evening. Clotilde rallied him on his
wish to be *incognito;* and he found himself on a
sudden, by a short train of natural events, in the
company of the person whom his mother intended
for his wife; the object of his affection whom he
had just discovered; and the interesting stranger
who had promised him an explanation relative to
the mysterious portraits.

Their society was soon augmented by the mistress of the *château*, in whom Ferdinand recognised one of those who sat by his side the preceding evening. In consideration for Emily, they omitted all the subjects most interesting to Ferdinand; but after supper the baron drew nearer to him.

" I doubt not," said he to him, " that you are anxious to have some light thrown on events, of which, according to your recital last night, you were a spectator. I knew you from the first; and I knew also, that the story you related as of a friend, was your own history. I cannot, however, inform you of more than I know: but that will perhaps be sufficient to save Emily, for whom I feel the affection of a daughter, from chagrin and uneasiness; and from your recital of last evening, I perceive you take a lively interest concerning her."

" Preserve Emily from uneasiness," replied Ferdinand with warmth; " explain yourself: what is there I ought to do?"

" We cannot," answered the baron, " converse here with propriety; to-morrow morning I will come and see you in your apartment."

Ferdinand asked him for an audience that night; but the baron was inflexible. " It is not my wish," said he, " to work upon your imagination by any marvellous recital, but to converse with you on the

very important concerns of two distinguished families. For which reason, I think the freshness of
morning will be better suited to lessen the horror
that my recital must cause you:, therefore, if not
inconvenient to you, I wish you to attend me at an
early hour in the morning: I am fond of rising with
the sun ; and yet I have never found the time till
mid-day too long for arranging my affairs," added
he, smiling, and turning half round towards the rest
of the party, as if speaking on indifferent topics.
. . Ferdinand passed a night of agitation, thinking
of the conference he was to have with the baron ;
who was at his window at dawn of day. " You
know," said the baron, " that I married the old count
of Wartbourg's sister; which alliance was less the
cause, than the consequence, of our intimate friendship. We reciprocally communicated our most
secret thoughts, and the one never undertook any
thing, without the other taking an equal interest
with himself in his projects. The count had, however, one secret from me, of which I should never
have come at the knowledge but for an accident.
. . " On a sudden, a report was spread abroad, that
the phantom of the Nun's rock had been seen,
which was the name given by the peasantry to the
old ruined tower which you knew. Persons of
sense only laughed at the report: I was anxious
the following night to unmask this spectre, and I

already anticipated my triumph : but to my no
small surprise, the count endeavoured to dissuade
me from the attempt; and the more I persisted, the
more serious his arguments became; and at length
he conjured me in the name of friendship to re-
linquish the design.

" His gravity of manner excited my attention ; I
asked him several questions; I even regarded his
fears in the light of disease, and urged him to take
suitable remedies : but he answered me with an air
of chagrin, ' Brother, you know my sincerity towards you ; but this is a secret sacred to my family.
My son can alone be informed of it, and that only
on my death-bed. Therefore ask me no more
questions.'

" I held my peace ; but I secretly collected all
the traditions known amongst the peasantry. The
most generally believed one was, that the phantom
of the Nun's rock was seen when any one of the
count's family were about to die ; and in effect, in
a few days after the count's youngest son expired.
The count seemed to apprehend it : he gave the
strictest possible charge to the nurse to take care
of him; and under pretext of feeling indisposed
himself, sent for two physicians to the castle : but
these extreme precautions were precisely the cause
of the child's death ; for the nurse passing over the
stones near the ruins, in her extreme care took the

child in her arms to carry him, and her foot slip-
ping, she fell, and in her fall wounded the child so
much, that he expired on the spot. She said she
fancied that she saw the child extended, bleeding
in the midst of the stones; that her fright had made
her fall with her face on the earth; and that when
she came to herself, the child was absolutely lying
weltering in his blood, precisely on the same spot
where she had seen his ghost.

"I will not tire you with a relation of all the
sayings uttered by an illiterate woman to explain
the cause of the vision, for under similar accidents
invention far outstrips reality. I could not expect
to gain much more satisfactory information from
the family records; for the principal documents
were preserved in an iron chest, the key of which
was never out of the possession of the owner of the
castle. I however discovered, by the genealogical
register and other similar papers, that this family
had never had collateral male branches; but further than this, my researches could not discover.

"At length, on my friend's death-bed I obtained
some information, which, however, was far from
being satisfactory. You remember, that while the
son was on his travels, the father was attacked by
the complaint which carried him off so suddenly.
The evening previous to his decease, he sent for
me express, dismissed all those who were with

him, and turning towards me, said : ' I am aware
that my end is fast approaching, and am the first
of my family that has been carried off without
communicating to his son the secret on which the
safety of our house depends. Swear to me to reveal
it only to my son, and I shall die contented.' · ι · :

" In the names of friendship and honour, I promised what he exacted of me, and he thus began :
" ' The origin of my race, as you know, is not to
be traced. : Ditmar, the first of my ancestry mentioned in the written records, accompanied the emperor Otho to Italy. His history is also very obscure. He had an enemy called count Bruno, whose
only son he killed in revenge, according to ancient
tradition, and then kept the father confined till his
death in that tower, whose ruins, situated in the
Nun's rock, still defy the hand of time. That portrait
which hangs alone, in the state-chamber, is Ditmar's ; and if the traditions of the family are to be
believed, it was painted by the Dead. In fact, it
is almost impossible to believe that any human
being could have contemplated sufficiently long to
paint the portrait, the outline of features so hideous.
My forefathers have frequently tried to plaster
over this redoubtable figure ; but in the night, the
colours came through the plaster, and re-appeared
as distinctly as before ; and often in the night, this
Ditmar has been seen wandering abroad dressed in

the garb represented in the picture; and by kissing
the descendants of the family, has doomed them to
death. Three of my children have received this
fatal kiss. It is said, a monk imposed on him
this penance in expiation of his crimes. But he
cannot destroy all the children of his race : for so
long as the ruins of the old tower shall remain,
and whilst one stone shall remain on another, so
long shall the count de Wartbourg's family exist ;
and so long shall the spirit of Ditmar wander on
earth, and devote to death the branches of his
house, without being able to annihilate the trunk.
His race will never be extinct; and his punishment
will only cease when the ruins of the tower are entirely dispersed. He brought up, with a truly paternal care, the daughter of his enemy, and wedded
her to a rich and powerful knight; but notwithstanding this, the monk never remitted his penance. Ditmar, however, foreseeing that one day
or other his race would perish, was certainly anxious ere then, to prepare for an event on which his
deliverance depended; and accordingly made a relative disposition of his hereditary property, in case
of his family becoming extinct. The act which
contained his will, was ratified by the emperor
Otho : as yet it has not been opened, and nobody
knows its contents. It is kept in the secret archives of our house.'

"The speaking thus much was a great effort to my friend. He required a little rest, but was shortly after incapable of articulating a single word. I performed the commission with which he charged me to his son."

"And he did, notwithstanding ——" replied Ferdinand.

"Even so," answered the baron: "but judge more favourably of your excellent friend. I have often seen him alone in the great state-chamber, with his eyes fixed on this horrible portrait: he would then go into the other rooms, where the portraits of his ancestors were ranged for several successive generations; and after contemplating them with visible internal emotion, would return to that of the founder of his house. Broken sentences, and fiequent soliloquies, which I overheard by accident, did not leave me a shadow of doubt, but that he was the first of his race who had magnanimity of soul sufficient to resolve on liberating the spirit of Ditmar from its penance, and of sacrificing himself to release his house from the malediction, that hung over it. Possibly he was strengthened in his resolutions by the grief he experienced for the death of his dearly beloved."

"Oh!" cried Ferdinand deeply affected, "how like my friend!"

"He had, however, in the ardour of his en-

thusiasm, forgotten to guard his sister's sensibility," said the baron.

" How so ?" demanded Ferdinand.

" It is in consequence of this," answered the
baron, " that I now address myself to you, and reveal to you the secret. I have told you that Ditmar demonstrated a paternal affection to the daughter of his enemy, had given her a handsome portion,
and had married her to a valiant knight. Learn
then, that this knight was Adelbert de Meltheim,
from whom the counts of this name descended in
a direct line."

" Is it possible ?" exclaimed Ferdinand, " the
author of my race !"

" The same," answered the baron ; " and according to appearances, Ditmar designed that the
family of Meltheim should succeed him on the
extinction of his own. Haste, then, in order to
establish your probable right to the ——"

" Never——" said Ferdinand " ——so long as
Emily——"

" This is no more than I expected from you,"
replied the baron; " but remember, that in Ditmar's time the girls were not thought of in deeds
of this kind. Your inconsiderate generosity would
be prejudicial to Emily. For the next of kin who
lay claim to the fief, do not probably possess very
gallant ideas."

" As a relation, though only on the female side,

I have taken the necessary measures; and I think it
right you should be present at the castle of Wartbourg when the seals are broken, that you may
be immediately recognised as the only immediate
descendant of Adelbert, and that you may take instant possession of the inheritance." .

" And Emily ?" demanded Ferdinand.

" As for what is to be done for her," replied the
baron, " I leave to you; and feel certain of her being provided for suitably, since her destiny will be
in the hands of a man whose birth equals her own,
who knows how to appreciate the rank in which
she is placed, and who will evince his claims to
merit and esteem."

" Have I a right, then," said Ferdinand, " to flat-
ter myself with the hope that Emily will permit
me to surrender her the property to which she is
actually entitled ?".

" Consult Emily on the subject," said the baron.
—And here finished the conference.

Ferdinand, delighted, ran to Emily. She answered with the same frankness he had manifested; and
they were neither of them slow to confess their
mutual passion.

Several days passed in this amiable delirium.
The inhabitants of the château participated in the
joy of the young lovers; and Ferdinand at length
wrote to his mother, to announce the choice he had
made.

They were occupied in preparations for removing to the castle of Wartbourg, when a letter arrived, which at once destroyed Ferdinand's happiness. His mother refused to consent to his marriage with Emily: her husband having, she said, on
his death-bed, insisted on his wedding the baron of
Hainthal's daughter, and that she should refuse her
consent to any other marriage. He had discovered
a family secret, which forced him peremptorily
to press this point, on which depended his son's
welfare, and the happiness of his family ; she had
given her promise, and was obliged to maintain it,
although much afflicted at being compelled to act
contrary to her son's inclinations.

In vain did Ferdinand conjure his mother to
change her determination ; he declared to her that
he would be the last of his race, rather than re-
nounce Emily. She was not displeased with his
entreaties, but remained inflexible.

The baron plainly perceived, from Ferdinand's
uneasiness and agitation, that his happiness had fled ;
and as he possessed his entire confidence, he soon
became acquainted with the cause of his grief. He
wrote in consequence to the countess Meltheim,
and expressed his astonishment at the singular
disposition the count had made on his death-bed :
but all he could obtain from her, was a promise to
come to the castle of Wartbourg, to see the fe-

male whom she destined for her son, and the one
whom he had himself chosen; and probably to
elucidate by her arrival, so singular and compli-
cated an affair.

,. Spring was beginning to enliven all nature, when
Ferdinand, accompanied by Emily, the Baron, and
his daughter, arrived at the castle of Wartbourg.
The preparations which the principal cause of their
journey required, occupied some days. Ferdinand
and Emily consoled themselves in the hope that
the countess of Meltheim's presence would remove
every obstacle which opposed their love, and that
at sight of the two lovers she would overcome her
scruples.

,. A few days afterwards she arrived, embraced
Emily in the most affectionate manner, and called
her, her dear daughter, at the same time expressing her great regret that she could not really
consider her such, being obliged to fulfil a promise
made to her dying husband.

:. The baron at length persuaded her to reveal the
motive for this singular determination : and after
deliberating a short time, she thus expressed herself :—

" The secret you are anxious I should reveal to
you, concerns your family, Monsieur le Baron :
consequently, if you release me from the necessity
of longer silence, I am very willing to abandon my

scruples. A fatal picture has, you know, robbed me of my daughter; and my husband, after this melancholy accident, determined on entirely removing this unfortunate portrait: he accordingly gave orders for it to be put in a heap of old furniture, where no one would think of looking for it; and in order to discover the best place to conceal it, he was present when it was taken there. In the removal, he perceived a piece of parchment behind the canvass, which the fall had a little damaged: having removed it, he discovered it to be an old document, of a singular nature. The original of this portrait, (said the deed,) was called Bertha de Hainthal; she fixes her looks on her female descendants, in order that if any one of them should receive its death by this portrait; it may prove, an expiatory sacrifice which will reconcile her to God. She will then see the families of Hainthal and Meltheim united by the bonds of love ; and finding herself released, she will have cause to rejoice in the birth of her after-born descendants.

" This then is the motive which made my husband anxious to fulfil, by the projected marriage, the vows of Bertha; for the death of his daughter, caused by Bertha, had rendered her very name formidable to him. You see, therefore, I have the same reasons for adhering to the promise, made my dying husband."

" Did not the count," demanded the baron, " allege any more positive reason for this command ?"

" Nothing more, most assuredly," replied the countess.

" Well then," answered the baron, " in case the writing of which you speak should admit of an explanation wholly differing from, but equally clear with, the one attached thereto by the deceased, would you sooner follow the sense than the letter of the writing ?"

" There is no doubt on that subject," answered the countess; " for no one is more anxious than myself to see that unfortunate promise set aside."

" Know then," said the baron, " that the corpse of that Bertha, who occasioned the death of your daughter, reposes here at Wartbourg; and that, on this subject, as well as all the other mysteries of the castle, we shall have our doubts satisfied."

The baron would not at this time explain himself further; but said to the countess, that the documents contained in the archives of the castle would afford the necessary information; and recommended that Ferdinand should, with all possible dispatch, hasten every thing relative to the succession. Conformable to the baron's wish, it was requisite that, previous to any other research, the secret deeds contained in the archives should be

opened. The law commissioners, and the next of kin
who were present, who, most likely, promised themselves an ample compensation for their curiosity
in the contents of the other parts of the records,
were anxious to raise objections; but the baron represented to them, that the secrets of the family
appertained to the unknown heir alone, and that
consequently no one 'had' a right to become acquainted with them, unless permitted by him... —

These reasons produced the proper effect. They
followed the baron into the immense vault in
which were deposited the family records. They
therein discovered an iron chest, which had not
been opened for nearly a thousand years. A mas-
sive chain, which several times wound round it,
was strongly fixed to the floor and to the wall; but
the emperor's grand seal was a greater security for
this sacred deposit, than all the chains and bolts
which guarded it. It was instantly recognised and
removed: the strong bolts yielded; and from the
chest was taken the old parchment which had resisted the effects of time. This piece contained,
as the baron expected, the disposition which confirmed the right of inheritance to the house of
Meltheim, in case of the extinction of the house of
Wartbourg: and Ferdinand, according to the baron's
advice, having in readiness the deeds justifying and
acknowledging him as the lawful heir to the house.

E

of Meltheim, the next of kin with regret permitted what they could not oppose; and he took possession of the inheritance. · The baron having made
him a signal, he immediately sealed the chest with
his seal. He afterwards entertained the strangers
in a splendid manner; and at night found himself
in possession of his castle, with only his mother,
Emily, the baron, and his daughter. . - . , . · :..·.·

" It will be but just," said the baron, " to devote this night, which introduces a new name into
this castle, to the memory of those who have
hitherto possessed it. And we shall acquit ourselves most suitably in this duty, by reading in the
council-chamber the documents which, without
doubt, are destined to explain, as supplementary
deeds, the will of Ditmar." · · · · :·. · · v·.   · ·

This arrangement was instantly adopted. The
hearts of Emily and Ferdinand were divided between hope and fear; for they impatiently, yet
doubtingly, awaited the denouement of Bertha's
history, which, after so many successive generations, had in so incomprehensible a manner inter-
fered with their attachment. · · · ·· · — ·   · · ·

The chamber was lighted : Ferdinand opened
the iron case; and the baron examined the old
parchments. · · ·   ·· ·· — - .·· ·— · ·

" This," cried he, after having searched some
short time, " will inform us." So saying, he drew

from the chest some sheets of parchment. On the
one which enveloped the rest was the portrait of
a knight of an agreeable figure, and habited in the
costume of the tenth century; and the inscription
at the bottom called him Ditmar; but they could
scarcely discover the slightest resemblance in it to
the frightful portrait in the state-chamber. · ·.· ·;
·. The baron offered to translate, in reading to them
the document written in Latin, provided they
would make allowances for the errors which were
likely to arise from so hasty a translation. The curiosity of his auditors was so greatly excited, that
they readily consented; and he then read as follows:
·· "I the undersigned Tutilon, monk of St. Gall,
have, with the lord Ditmar's consent, written the
following narrative: I have omitted nothing, nor
written aught of my own accord. ·., ·.· ·(· ·
· "Being sent for to Metz, to carve in stone the
image of the Virgin Mary; and that mother of our
blessed Saviour having opened my eyes and directed my hands, so that I could contemplate her celestial countenance, and represent it on stone to be
worshipped by true believers, the lord Ditmar discovered me, and engaged me to follow him to his
castle, in order that I might execute his portrait
for his descendants. I began painting it in the
state-chamber of his castle; and on returning the
following day to resume my task, I found that a

strange hand had been at work, and had given to
the portrait quite a different countenance, which
was horrible to look at, for it resembled one who
had risen from the dead. I trembled with terror:
however, I effaced these hideous features, and I
painted anew the count Ditmar's figure, according
to my recollection; but the following day I again
discovered the nocturnal labour of the stranger
hand. I was seized with still greater fear, but resolved to watch during the night; and I recom-
menced painting the knight's figure, such as it really
was. At midnight I took a torch, and advancing
softly into the chamber to examine the portrait, I
perceived a spectre resembling the skeleton of a
child; it held a pencil, and was endeavouring to give
Ditmar's image the hideous features of death.

" On my entering, the spectre slowly turned its
head towards me, that I might see its frightful
visage. My terror became extreme: I advanced no
further, but retired to my room, where I remained
in prayer till morning; for I was unwilling to interrupt the work executed in the dead of night. In
the morning, discovering the same strange features
in Ditmar's portrait as that of the two preceding
mornings, I did not again risk effacing the work of
the nightly painter; but went in search of the
knight, and related to him what I had seen. I
shewed him the picture. He trembled with hor-

ror, and confessed his crimes to me, for which he
required absolution. . Having for three successive
days, invoked all the saints to my assistance, I imposed on him as a penance for the murder of his
enemy, which he had avowed to me, to submit to
the most rigid mortifications in a dungeon during
the rest of his life. But I told him, that as he had
murdered an innocent child, his spirit would never
be at rest till it had witnessed the extermination of
his race ; for the Almighty would punish the death
of that child by the death of the children of Ditmar, who, with the exception of one in each generation, would all be carried off in early life; and
as for him, his spirit would wander during the
night, resembling the portrait painted by the hand
of the skeleton child; and that he would condemn to
death, by a kiss, the children who were the sacri-
fices to his crimes, in the same manner as he had
given one to his enemy's child before he killed it :
and that, in fine, his race should not become extinct, so long as stone remained on stone in the
tower where he had permitted his enemy to die of
hunger. I then gave him absolution. He immediately made over his seigniory to his son ; and
married the daughter of his enemy, who had been
brought up by him, to the brave knight Sir Adalbert. He bequeathed all his property, in case of
his race becoming extinct, to this knight's descend-

ants, and caused this will to be ratified by the emperor Otho. After having done so, he retired to a
cave near the tower, where his corpse is interred ;
for he died like a pious recluse, and expiated his
crimes by extreme penance. As soon as he was
laid in his coffin, he resembled the portrait in the
state-chamber; but during his life he was like the
portrait depicted on this parchment, which I was
able to paint without interruption, after having
given him absolution: and by his command I have
written and signed this document since his death;
and I deposit it, with the emperor's letters pa-
tent, in an iron chest, which I have caused to be
sealed. I pray God speedily to deliver his soul;
and to cause his body to rise from the dead to
everlasting felicity!" .

" He is delivered," cried Emily, greatly affected;
" and his image will no longer spread terror
around. But I confess that the sight of that figure,
and even that of the frightful portrait itself, would
never have led me to dream of such horrible
crimes as the monk Tutilon relates. Certain I
am, his enemy must have mortally wounded his
happiness, or he undoubtedly would have been incapable of committing such frightful crimes.".

" Possibly," said the baron, continuing his researches, " we shall discover some explanation on
that point.",

" We must also find some respecting Bertha,"
replied Ferdinand in a low tone, and casting a ti-
mid look on Emily and his mother.

" This night," answered the baron, " is consecrated to the memory of the dead; let us therefore
forget our own concerns, since those of the past
call our attention."

" Assuredly," exclaimed Emily, " the unfortunate person who secured these sheets in the chest,
ardently looked forward to the hope of their coming to light; let us therefore delay it no longer."

The baron, after having examined several, read
aloud these words:

" The confession of Ditmar." And he continued
thus :—" Peace and health. When this sheet is
drawn from the obscurity in which it is now buried,
my soul, will, I hope firmly in God and the saints,
be at eternal rest and peace. But for your good
I have ordered to be committed to paper the
cause of my chastisement, in order that you may
learn that vengeance belongs to God alone, and
not to men; for the most just amongst them knows
not how to judge: and again, that you may not in
your heart condemn me, but rather that you may
pity me; for my misery has nearly equalled my
crimes; and my spirit would never have dreamt of
evil, if man had not rent my heart."

·" How justly," · · exclaimed Ferdinand, ·" has
Emily's good sense divined thus much !" ·   ·   ·

The baron continued : ·" My name is Ditmar;·
they surnamed me The Rich, though I was then
only a poor knight, and my only possession was a·
very small castle. ·When the emperor Otho departed for Italy, whither he was called by· the·
beautiful Adelaide to receive her hand, I followed
him; and I gained the affection of the most charming woman in Pavia, whom I conducted as my in-
tended·spouse to the castle of my forefathers. Al-·
ready the day appointed for the celebration of my
nuptials was at hand : the emperor sent for me.
His favourite, the count Bruno de Hainthal had
seen Bertha —" · ·   ·   · ·— · ·

· ·" Bertha !" exclaimed every one present. ·But·
the baron, without permitting them to interrupt
him, continued his translation.   ·   ·   ·

·"·" One day, when the emperor had promised to
grant him any recompence that he thought his ser-
vices merited, he asked of him my intended bride.
Otho was mute with astonishment ;—but his imperial word was given. I presented myself before
the emperor, who offered me riches, lands, ho-
nours, if I would but consent to yield Bertha to the
count : but she was dearer to me than every
worldly good. The emperor yielded to a torrent of

anger: he carried off my intended bride by force,
ordered my castle to be pulled down, and caused
me to be thrown into prison.

"I cursed his power and my destiny. The amiable figure of Bertha, however, appeared to me
in a dream ; and I consoled myself during the day
by the sweet illusions of the night. At length my
keeper said to me: 'I pity you, Ditmar; you suffer
in a prison for your fidelity, while Bertha aban-
dons you. To-morrow she weds the count : accede then to the emperor's wish, ere it be too
late ; and ask of him what you think fit, as a recompence for the loss of the faithless fair.' These
words froze my heart. The following night, instead of the gracious image of Bertha, the frightful spirit of vengeance presented itself to me. The
following morning I said to my keeper: Go and tell
the emperor, I yield Bertha to his Bruno ; but as
a recompence, I demand this tower, and as much
land as will be requisite to build me a new castle.'
The emperor was satisfied ; for he frequently repented his violent passions, but he could not alter
what he had already decided. He therefore gave
me the tower in which I had been confined, and all
the lands around it for the space of four leagues.
He also gave me more gold and silver than was
sufficient to build a castle much more magnificent
than the one he had caused to be pulled down. I

took unto myself a wife, in order to perpetuate my
race; but Bertha still reigned sole mistress of my
heart. I also built myself a castle, from which I
made a communication, by subterranean and secret
passages, with my former prison the tower, and
with the castle of Bruno, the residence of my mor-
tal enemy. As soon as the edifice was completed,
I entered the fortress by the secret passage, and
appeared as the spirit of one of his ancestors before the bed of his son, the heir with which Bertha had presented him. The women who lay be-
side him were seized with fear: I leaned over the
child, who was the precise image of its mother,
and kissed its forehead; but—it was the kiss of
death; it carried with it a secret poison.

"Bruno and Bertha acknowledged the vengeance of Heaven: they received it as a punishment
for the wrongs they had occasioned me; and they
devoted their first child to the service of God. As
it was a girl, I spared it: but Bertha had no
more children; and Bruno, irritated to find his race
so nearly annihilated, repudiated his wife, as if he
repented the injustice of which he had been guilty
in taking her, and married another. The unfortunate Bertha took refuge in a monastery, and consecrated herself to Heaven: but her reason fled; and
one night she quitted her retreat, came to the tower
in which I had been confined in consequence of

her perfidy, there bewailed her crime, and there
grief terminated her existence; which circumstance
gave rise to that tower being called the Nun's
Rock. I heard, during the night, her sobs; and on
going to the tower found Bertha extended motion-
less; the dews of night had seized her :—she was
dead. I then resolved to avenge her loss. I placed
her corpse in a deep vault beneath the tower; and
having by means of my subterranean passage discovered all the count's movements, I attacked him
when unguarded; and dragging him to the vault
which contained his wife's corpse, I there abandoned him. The emperor, irritated against him for
having divorced Bertha, gave me all his possessions,
as a remuneration for the injustice I had heretofore
experienced.

"I caused all the subterranean passages to be
closed. I took under my care his daughter Hildegarde, and brought her up as my child : she
loved the count Adalbert de Meltheim. But one
night her mother's ghost appeared to her, and re-
minded her that she was consecrated to the Almighty: this vision, however, could not deter
her from marrying Adalbert. The night of her
marriage the phantom appeared again before her
bed, and thus addressed her :

"'Since you have infringed the vow I made, my

spirit can never be at rest, till one of your female
descendants receives its death from me.'

" This discourse occasioned me to send for the
venerable Tutilon, monk of St. Gall, who was very
celebrated, in order that he might paint a portrait
of Bertha, as she had painted herself in the monastery during her insanity; and I gave it to her
daughter.

" Tutilon concealed behind that portrait a
writing on parchment, the contents of which were
as follows :

" ' I am Bertha ; and I look at my daughters, to
see whether one of them will not die for me, in
expiation of my crimes, and thus reconcile me to
God. Then shall I see the two families of Meltheim and Hainthal reunited by love, and in the birth
of their descendants I shall enjoy happiness.' "

" This then," exclaimed Ferdinand; " is the fatal writing that is to separate me from Emily; but
which, in fact, only unites me to her more firmly !
and Bertha, delivered from her penance, blesses
the alliance ; for by my marriage with Emily, the
descendants of Bertha and Ditmar will be reunited."

" Do you think," demanded the baron of the
countess, " that this explanation can admit of the
slightest doubt ?"

The only answer the countess made, was by embracing Emily, and placing her hand in that of her son.

The joy was universal. Clotilde in particular had an air of extreme delight; and her father several times, in a jocular manner, scolded her for expressing her joy so vehemently. The following morning they moved the seals from the state-chamber, in order to contemplate the horrible portrait with somewhat less of sadness than heretofore : but they found that it had faded in a singular manner, and the colours, which formerly appeared so harsh, had blended and become softened.

Shortly after arrived the young man who was anxious to enter into an argument with Ferdinand on the explication of the mysteries relative to the portraits. Clotilde did not conceal that he was far from indifferent to her; and they discovered the joy she had evinced, in discovering the favourable turn Emily's attachment had taken, was not altogether disinterested, but occasioned by the prospect it afforded of happiness to herself. Her father, in fact, would never have approved her choice, had not the countess Meltheim removed all pretensions to Clotilde.

" But," asked Ferdinand of Clotilde's intended, " do you not forgive our having searched into certain mysteries which concerned us ?"

"Completely," he answered; "but not less dis-
interestedly, than formerly, when I maintained a
contrary opinion. I ought now to confess to you,
that I was present at the fatal accident which
caused your sister's death, and that I then discovered the writing concealed behind the portrait.
I naturally explained it as your father did afterwards; but I held my peace; for the consequences
have brought to light what the discovery of that
writing had caused me to apprehend for my love."

"Unsatisfactory explanations are bad," replied
Ferdinand, laughing.

The happy issue of these discoveries spread
universal joy amongst the inhabitants of the castle,
which was in some degree heightened by the
beauty of the season. The lovers were anxious to
celebrate their marriage ere the fall of the leaf.
And when next the primrose's return announced
the approach of spring, Emily gave birth to a
charming boy.

Ferdinand's mother, Clotilde and her husband,
and all the friends of the family, among whom
were the pastor who was so fond of music, and
his pretty little wife, assembled at the *fête* given in
honour of the christening. When the priest who
was performing the ceremony asked what name he
was to give the child, that of Ditmar was uttered
by every mouth, as if they had previously agreed on

it. The christening over, Ferdinand, elate with joy, accompanied by his relations and guests, carried his son to the state-chamber, before his forefather's portrait; but it was no longer perceptible; the colours, figure,—all had disappeared; not the slightest trace remained...

II.

THE FATED HOUR.

———— " Wan the maiden was,
Of saintly paleness, and there seem'd to dwell
In the strong beauties of her countenance
Something that was not earthly."
SOUTHEY'S JOAN OF ARC.

" The clock has toll'd; and, hark! the bell
Of death beats slow." MASON'S ELEGIES.

A HEAVY rain prevented the three friends from
taking the morning's walk they had concerted: notwithstanding which, Amelia and Maria failed not
to be at Florentina's house at the appointed hour.
The latter had for some time past been silent,
pensive, and absorbed in thought; and the anxiety
of her friends made them very uneasy at the visible
impression left on her mind by the violent tempest
of the preceding night.

Florentina met her friends greatly agitated, and
embraced them with more than usual tenderness.

" Fine weather for a walk!" cried Amelia: "how
have you passed this dreadful night?"

" Not very well, you may easily imagine. My
residence is in too lonely a situation."

" Fortunately," replied Maria, laughing, " it will not long be yours."

" That's true," answered Florentina, sighing deeply. : " The count returns from his travels to-morrow, in the hope of soon conducting me to the altar."

" Merely in the hope ?" replied Maria : " the mysterious manner in which you uttered these words, leads me to apprehend you mean to frustrate those hopes."

" I ?——— But how frequently in this life does hope prove only an untimely flower ?"

" My dear Florentina," said Maria, embracing her, " for some time past my sister and I have vainly attempted to account for your lost gaiety; and have been tormented with the idea, that possibly family reasons have induced you, contrary to your wishes, to consent to this marriage which is about to take place."

" Family reasons ! Am I not then the last of our house ; the only remaining one, whom the tombs of my ancestors have not as yet enclosed ? And have I not for my Ernest that ardent affection: which is natural to my time of life ? Or do you think me capable of such duplicity, when I have so recently depicted to you, in the most glowing colours, the man of my heart's choice ?"

" What then am I to believe ?" inquired Maria.

F

"Is it not a strange contradiction, that a young girl, handsome and witty, rich and of high rank, and who, independently of these advantages, will not by her marriage be estranged from her family, should approach the altar with trembling?"

Florentina, holding out her hand to the two sisters, said to them:

"How kind you are! I ought really to feel quite ashamed in not yet having placed entire confidence in your friendship, even on a subject which is to me, at this moment, incomprehensible. At this moment I am not equal to the task; but in the course of the day I hope to be sufficiently recovered. In the mean while let us talk on less interesting subjects."

The violent agitation of Florentina's mind was so evident at this moment, that the two sisters willingly assented to her wishes. Thinking that the present occasion required trifling subjects of conversation, they endeavoured to joke with her on the terrors of the preceding night. However, Maria finished by saying, with rather a serious air,—

"I must confess, that more than once I have been tempted to think something extraordinary occurred. At first it appeared as if some one opened and shut the window of the room in which we slept, and then as if they approached my bed. I distinctly heard footsteps: an icy trembling seized me, and I covered my face over with the clothes."

"Alas!" exclaimed Amelia, "I cannot tell you how frequently I have heard similar noises. But as yet nothing have I seen."

"Most fervently do I hope," replied Florentina in an awful tone of voice, "that neither of you will ever, in this life, be subject to a proof of this nature!"

The deep sigh which accompanied these words, and the uneasy look she cast on the two sisters, produced evident emotions in them both.

"Possibly *you* have experienced such proof?" replied Amelia.

"Not precisely so: but —— suspend your curiosity. This evening——if I am still alive——I mean to say—that this evening I shall be better able to communicate all to you."

Maria made a sign to Amelia, who instantly understood her sister; and thinking that Florentina wished to be alone, though evidently disturbed in her mind, they availed themselves of the first opportunity which her silence afforded. Her prayerbook was lying open on the table, which, now perceiving for the first time, confirmed Maria in the idea she had conceived. In looking for her shawl she removed a handkerchief which covered this book, and saw that the part which had most pro-

bably occupied Florentina before their arrival
was the Canticle on Death. The three friends separated, overcome and almost weeping, as if they
were never to meet again.

Amelia and Maria awaited with the greatest impatience the hour of returning to Florentina.—
They embraced her with redoubled satisfaction,
for she seemed to them more gay than usual.

" My dear girls," said she to them, " pardon, I
pray you, my abstraction of this morning. De-
pressed by having passed so bad a night, I thought
myself on the brink of the grave ; and fancied it
needful to make up my accounts in this world, and
prepare for the next. I have made my will, and
have placed it in the magistrate's hands : however,
since I have taken a little repose this afternoon, 1
find myself so strong, and in such good spirits, that
I feel as if I had escaped the danger which threatened me."

" But, my dear," replied Maria, in a mild yet
affectionate tone of reproach, " how could one
sleepless night fill your mind with such gloomy
thoughts ?"

" I agree with you on the folly of permitting it
so to do ; and had I encouraged sinister thoughts,
that dreadful night would not have been the sole
cause, for it found me in such a frame of mind
that its influence was not at all necessary to add to

my horrors. ; But no more of useless mystery. I
will fulfil my promise, and 'clear up your doubts
on many parts of my manner and conduct, which
at present must appear to you inexplicable. Prepare yourselves for the strangest and most surprising events.—But the damp and cold evening air has
penetrated this room, it will therefore be better to
have a fire lighted, that the chill which my recital
may produce be not increased by any exterior
cause."

While they were lighting the fire, Maria and
her sister expressed great joy at seeing such a
happy change in Florentina's manner; and the latter could scarcely describe the satisfaction she felt,
at having resolved to develop to them the secret
which she had so long concealed.

The three friends being alone, Florentina began
as follows :—

" You were acquainted with my sister Seraphina, whom I had the misfortune to lose; but I
alone can boast of possessing her confidence; which
is the cause of my mentioning many things relative
to her, before I begin the history I have promised,
in which she is the principal personage.

" From her infancy, Seraphina was remarkable
for several singularities. She was a year younger
than myself; but frequently, while seated by her
side I was amusing myself with the playthings

common to our age, she would fix her eyes, by the
half hour together, as if absorbed in thought : she
seldom took any part in our infantine amusements.
This disposition greatly chagrined our parents; for
they attributed Seraphina's indifference to stupid-
ity; and they were apprehensive this defect would
necessarily prove an obstacle in the education requisite for the distinguished rank we held in society, my father being, next the prince, the first
person in the country. They had already thought
of procuring for her a canonry from some noble
chapel, when things took an entirely different turn.

" Her preceptor, an aged man, to whose care
they had confided her at a very early age, assured
them, that in his life he had never met with so
astonishing an intellect as Seraphina's. My father
doubted the assertion : but an examination, which
he caused to be made in his presence, convinced
him that it was founded in truth.

" Nothing was then neglected to give Seraphina
every possible accomplishment :—masters of different languages, of music, and of dancing, every day
filled the house.

" But in a short time my father perceived that
he was again mistaken : for Seraphina made so
little progress in the study of the different languages, that the masters shrugged their shoulders;
and the dancing-master pretended, that though her

feet were extremely pretty, he could do nothing
with them, as her head seldom took the trouble to
guide them.

" By way of retaliation, she made such wonderful progress in music that she soon excelled her
masters. She sang in a manner superior to that
of the best opera-singers.

" My father acknowledged that his plans for
the education of this extraordinary child were now
as much too enlarged, as they were before too cir-
cumscribed ; and that it would not do to keep too
tight a hand over her, but let her follow the impulse of her own wishes.

" This new arrangement afforded Seraphina the
opportunity of more particularly studying the science
of astronomy ; which was one they had never thought
of as needful for her. You can, my friends, form
but a very indifferent idea of the avidity with
which (if so I may express myself) she devoured
those books which treated on celestial bodies ; or
what rapture the globes and telescopes occasioned
her, when her father presented them to her on her
thirteenth birth-day.

" But the progress made in this science in our days
did not long satisfy Seraphina's curiosity. To my
father's great grief, she was wrapped up in reveries
of astrology ; and more than once she was found
in the morning occupied in studying books which

treated on the influence of the stars, and which she
had begun to peruse the preceding evening.

" My mother, being at the point of death, was
anxious, I believe, to remonstrate with Seraphina
on this whim ; but her death was too sudden. My
father thought that at this tender age Seraphina's
whimsical fancy would wear off: however, time
passed on, and he found that she still remained
constant to a study she had cherished from her infancy.

" You cannot forget the general sensation her
beauty produced at court : how much the fashion-
able versifiers of the day sang her graceful figure
and beautiful flaxen locks ; and how often they
failed, when they attempted to describe the particular and indefinable character which distinguished
her fine blue eyes. I must say, I have often embraced my sister, whom I loved with the greatest
affection, merely to have the pleasure of getting
nearer, if possible, to her soft angelic eyes, from
which Seraphina's pale countenance borrowed almost all its sublimity.

" She received many extremely advantageous
proposals of marriage, but declined them all. You
know her predilection in favour of solitude, and
that she never went out but to enjoy my society.
She took no pleasure in dress ; nay, she even
avoided all occasions which required more than or-

dinary;expense. ., Those who, were, not acquainted
with the ,singularity of her; character, might. have
accused, her of affectation. , : , .. . ,' .. l., . ,.
. ,": But a very extraordinary particularity,, which
I, by chance discovered, in her just as, she, attained her fifteenth year, created an impression, of
'fear on my ,mind; which; will never, be effaced.' ·'
. ,"On;my return, from making a visit,;,I, found
Seraphina in my father's cabinet, near the window,
with her eyes fixed and immoveable. Accustomed
from her earliest infancy;to 'see her' in this, situation, without being perceived by her I pressed her.
to my bosom, without producing on her,the least
sensation of my presence.; At, this; moment, I
looked, towards the garden, and I there saw, my
father walking with this same Seraphina whom I
held in my arms. . ., ...' . , , ' ., ..., ,'.. .'.
. ,," In the; name of God, my sister ——!" exclaimed I, equally cold with the statue before me;
who. now began to recover. ... . . .' . .: .. · '

" At the, same time my eye involuntarily. re-'
turned towards the garden, where I had, seen her;
and there perceived my father alone, looking, with
uneasiness, as it appeared to me, for her, who, but
an instant, before, was with him. · I endeavoured
to conceal this event from my sister ; but in, the,
most, affectionate tone she loaded me with questions to learn the cause of my agitation. ', : .. ,. (

"I eluded them as well as I could; and asked her how long she had been in the closet. She answered me, smiling, that I ought to know best; as she came in after me; and that if she was not mistaken, she had before that been walking in the garden with my father.

"This ignorance of the situation in which she was but an instant before, did not astonish me on my sister's account, as she had often shewn proofs of this absence of mind. At that instant my father came in, exclaiming: 'Tell me, my dear Seraphina, how you so suddenly escaped from my sight, and came here? We were, as you know, conversing; and scarcely had you finished speaking, when, looking round, I found myself alone. I naturally thought that you had concealed yourself in the adjacent thicket; but in vain I looked there for you; and on coming into this room, here I find you.'

"'It is really strange,' replied Seraphina; 'I know not myself how it has happened.'

"From that moment I felt convinced of what I had heard from several persons, but what my father always contradicted; which was, that while Seraphina was in the house, she had been seen elsewhere. I secretly reflected also on what my sister had repeatedly told me, that when a child (she was ignorant whether sleeping or awake), she

had been transported to heaven, where she had
played with angels; to which incident she attributed her disinclination to all infantine games.

" My father strenuously combated this idea, as
well as the event to which I had been witness, of
her sudden disappearance from the garden.

" ' Do not torment me any longer,' said he, ' with
these phænomena, which appear complaisantly re-
newed every day, in order to gratify your eager
imagination. It is true, that your sister's person
and habits present many singularities; but all your
idle talk will never persuade me that she holds any
immediate intercourse with the world of spirits.'

" My father did not then know, that where there
is any doubt of the future, the weak mind of man
ought not to allow him to profane the word *never*,
by uttering it.

" About a year and half afterwards, an event
occurred which had power to shake even my father's determined manner of thinking to its very
foundation. It was on a Sunday, that Seraphina
and I wished at last to pay a visit which we had
from time to time deferred: for notwithstanding
my sister was very fond of being with me, she
avoided even my society whenever she could not
enjoy it but in the midst of a large assembly,
where constraint destroyed all pleasure.

" To adorn herself for a party, was to her an

anticipated torment ; for she said, she only sub-
mitted to this trouble to please those whose frivolous and dissipated characters greatly offended
her. ' On similar occasions she sometimes met
with persons to whom she could not speak without
shuddering, and whose presence made her ill for
several days. '

" The hour of assembling approached; she was
anxious that I should go without her: my father
doubting her, came into our room, and insisted on
her changing her determination.

" ' I cannot permit you to infringe every duty.'

" He accordingly desired her to dress as quickly
as possible, and accompany me.

" The waiting-maid was just gone out on an er-
rand with which I had commissioned her. My
sister took a light to fetch her clothes from a
wardrobe in the upper story. She remained much
longer absent than was requisite. At length she
returned without a light :—I screamed with fright.
My father asked her in an agitated manner, what
had happened to her. In fact, she had scarcely
been absent a quarter of an hour, and yet during
that time her face had undergone a complete al-
teration ; her habitual paleness had given place to
a death-like hue; her ruby lips were turned blue.

" My arms involuntarily opened to embrace this
sister whom I adored. I almost doubted my sight,

for I could get no answer from her ; but for a long
while she leaned against my bosom, mute and inanimate. The look, replete with infinite softness,
which she gave my father and me, alone informed
us, that during her continuance in this incomprehensible trance,' she still belonged to the material
world.

"'I was seized with a sudden indisposition,' she
at length said in a low voice; ' but I now find myself better.'

" She, asked my father whether he still wished
her to go into society. He thought, that after an
occurrence of this nature her going out might be
dangerous: but he would not dispense with my
making the visit, although I endeavoured to persuade him that my attention might be needful to
Seraphina. I left her with an aching heart.

" I had ordered the carriage to be sent for me
at a very early hour : but the extreme anxiety I
felt would not allow me to wait its arrival, and I
returned home on foot. The servant could scarcely
keep pace with me, such was my haste to return to
Seraphina.

" On my arrival in her room, my impatience
was far from being relieved.

" ' Where is she ?' I quickly asked.

'," ' Who mademoiselle ?'

" ' Why, Seraphina.'

"' Mademoiselle, Seraphina is in your father's closet.'

"'-Alone ?'

"' No with his excellency.'

. " I ran to the boudoir: the door, which was previously shut, at that instant opened, and my father with Seraphina came out : the latter was in tears. I remarked that my father had an air of chagrin and doubt which not even the storms of public life had ever produced in his countenance.

" He made us a sign full of gentleness, and Seraphina followed me into another room : but she first assured my father she would remember the promise he had exacted, and of which I was still ignorant.

" Seraphina appeared to me so tormented by the internal conflicts she endured, that I several times endeavoured, but in vain, to draw from her the mysterious event which had so recently thrown her into so alarming a situation. At last I overcame her scruples, and she answered me as follows:

" ' Your curiosity shall be satisfied, in part. I will develop some of the mystery to you; but only on one irrevocable condition.'

" I entreated her instantly to name the condition : and she thus continued :—

" ' Swear to me, that you will rest satisfied with what I shall disclose to you, and that you will

never urge nor use that power which you possess
over my heart, to obtain a knowledge of what. I
am obliged to conceal from you.'

" I swore it to her.,

" ' Now, my dear Florentina, forgive me, if, for
the first time in my life, I have a secret from you;
and also for not being satisfied with your mere word
for the promise I have exacted from you. My father, to whom I have confided every thing, has imposed these two obligations on me, and his last
words were to that effect.'

'. " I begged her to come to the point.

" ' Words are inadequate to describe,' said she,
' the weight I felt my soul oppressed with when
I went to get my clothes. I had no sooner closed
the door of the room in which you and my father
were, than I fancied I was about to be separated
from life and all that constituted my happiness;
and that I had many dreadful nights to linger
through, ere I could arrive at a better and more
peaceful abode., The air which I breathed on the
staircase was not such as usually circulates around
us; it oppressed my breathing, and caused large
drops of icy perspiration to fall from my forehead.
Certain it is, I was not alone on the staircase; but
for a long while I dared not look around me.

" ' You know, my dear Florentina, with what
earnestness I wished and prayed, but in vain, that

my mother would appear to me after her death, if
only for once. I fancied that on the stairs I heard
my mother's spirit behind me. I was apprehensive it was come to punish me for the vows I had
already made.'

" ' A strange thought, certainly !'

" ' But how could I imagine that a mother, who
was goodness itself, could be offended by the natural wishes of a tenderly beloved child, or have
imputed them to indiscreet curiosity? It was no
less foolish to think that she, who had been so long
since enclosed in the tomb, should occupy herself
in inflicting chastisement on me, for faults which
were nearly obliterated from my recollection. I
was so immediately convinced of the weakness of
giving way to such ideas, that I summoned courage
and turned my head.

" ' Although my affrighted survey could discover
nothing, I again heard the footsteps following me,
but more distinctly than before. At the door of
the room I was about to enter, I felt my gown
held. Overpowered by terror, I was unable to
proceed, and fell on the threshold of the door.

" ' I lost no time, however, in reproaching myself for suffering terror so to overcome me ; and
recollected that there was nothing supernatural in
this accident, for my gown had caught on the
handle of an old piece of furniture which had been

placed in the passage, to be taken out of the house
the following day.

." ' This discovery inspired me with fresh courage.
I approached the wardrobe:, but judge my consternation, when, preparing to open it, the two doors
unclosed of themselves, without making the slightest
noise; the lamp which I held in my hand was extinguished, and—as if I was standing before a look-
ing-glass,—my exact image came out of the wardrobe: the light which it spread, illumined great
part of the room.

. " ' I then heard these words :—Why tremble you at the sight of your own spirit, which
appears to give you warning of your approaching
dissolution, and to reveal to you the fate of your
house ?'

" ' The phantom then informed me of several future events. But when, after having deeply medi-
tated on its prophetic words, I asked a question relative to you, the room became as dark as before,
and the spirit had vanished. This, my dear, is all
I am permitted to reveal.'.

" ' Your approaching death !' cried I :—That
thought had in an instant effaced all other.

" Smiling, she made me a sign in the affirma-
tive; and gave me to understand, at the same time,
that I ought to press her no further on this subject.
' My father,' added she, ' has promised to make you

G

acquainted, in proper time, with all it concerns you
to know.'

" ' At a proper time !' repeated I, in a plaintive
voice; for it appeared to me, that since I had
learned so much, it was high time that I should
be made acquainted with the whole. '

" The same evening I mentioned my wishes to
my father: but he was inexorable. He fancied that
possibly what had happened to Seraphina might
have arisen from her disordered and. overheated
imagination. However, three days afterwards, my
sister finding herself so ill as to be obliged to keep
her bed, my father's doubts began to be shaken; and
although the precise day of Seraphina's death had
not been named to me, I could not avoid observing
by her paleness, and the more than usually affectionate manner of embracing my father and me, that the
time of our eternal separation was not far off.

" ' Will the clock soon strike nine ?' asked Seraphina, while we were sitting near her bed in the
evening.

" ' Yes, soon,' replied my father.

" ' Well then !. think of me, dear objects of my
affection:—we shall meet again.' She pressed our
hands ; and the clock no sooner struck, than she
fell back in her bed, never to rise more.

" My father has since related to me every particular as it happened ; for at that time I was so

much, overcome that my senses had forsaken me.

"Seraphina's eyes were scarcely closed, when I returned to a life which then appeared to me insupportable. I was apprehensive that the state of stupefaction into which I was thrown by the dread of the loss that threatened me, had appeared to my sister a want of attachment. And from that time I have never thought of the melancholy scene without experiencing a violent shuddering.

"'You must be aware,' said my father to me (it was at the precise hour, and before the same chimney we are at this moment placed)—you must be aware, that the pretended vision should still be kept quite secret.' I was of his opinion; but could not help adding, 'What! still, my father, though one part of the prediction has in so afflicting a manner been verified, you continue to call it a pretended vision ?'

"'Yes, my child; you know not what a dangerous enemy to man is his own imagination. Seraphina will not be the last of its victims.'

"We were seated, as I before said, just as we now are; and I was about to name a motive which I had before omitted, when I perceived that his eyes were fixed in a disturbed manner on the door. I was ignorant of the cause, and could discover nothing extraordinary there: notwithstand-

ing, however, an instant afterwards it opened óf its
own accord."

. Here Florentina stopped, as if overcome anew
by the remembrance of her terror. At the same
moment Amelia rose from her seat uttering a loud
scream.

 ; Her sister and her friend inquired what ailéd
her. For a long while she made them no reply;
and would not resume her seat on the chair, the
back of which was towards the door. At length,
however, she confessed (casting an inquiring and
anxious look around her) that a hand, cold as ice,
had touched her neck.

 " This is truly the effect of imagination," said
Maria, reseating herself. " It was my hand : for
some time my arm has been resting on your chair;
and when mention was made of the door opening
of its own accord, I felt a wish to rest on some
living object—"

 " But à-propos,—And the door —— ?".

 " Strange incident ! I trembled with fear ; and
clinging to my father, asked him if he did not see
a sort of splendid light, a something brilliant, pe-
netrate the apartment.

 " ' 'Tis well !' answered he, in a low and tremu-
lous voice, ' we have lost a being whom we cherished ; and consequently, in some degree, our
minds are disposed to exalted ideas, and our ima-

gmations may very easily be duped by the same
illusions: besides, there is nothing very unnatural
in a door opening of its own accord.'

" 'It ought to be closely shut now,' replied I;
without having the courage to do it.

'Tis very easy to shut it,' said my father.
But he rose in visible apprehension, walked a
few paces, and then returned, adding, "The door
may remain open; for the room is too warm."

"It is impossible for me to describe, even by
comparison, the singular light I had perceived:
and I do assure you, that if, instead of the light, I
had seen my sister's spirit enter, I should have
opened my arms to receive it; for it was only the
mysterious and vague appearance of this strange
vision which caused me so much fear.

"The servants coming in at this instant with
supper, put an end to the conversation.

"Time could not efface the remembrance of
Seraphina; but it wore off all recollection of the
last apparition. My daily intercourse with you,
my friends, since the loss of Seraphina, has been
for me a fortunate circumstance, and has insensibly become an indispensable habit. I no longer
thought deeply of the prediction relative to our
house, uttered by the phantom to my sister; and
in the arms of friendship gave myself up entirely to

the innocent gaiety which youth inspires. The
beauties of spring contributed to the restoration of
my peace of mind. One evening, just as you had
left me, I continued walking in the garden, as if
intoxicated with the delicious vapours emitted from
the flowers, and the magnificent spectacle which
the serenity of the sky presented to my view.

" Absorbed entirely by the enjoyment of my
existence, I did not notice that it was later than
my usual hour for returning. And I know not
why, but that evening no one appeared to think of
me; for my father, whose solicitude for every thing
concerning me was redoubled since my sister's
death, and who knew I was in the garden, had not,
as was his usual custom, sent me any garment to
protect me from the chilling night air.

" While thus reflecting, I was seized with a violent feverish shivering, which I could by no means
attribute to the night air. My eyes accidentally
fixed on the flowering shrubs; and the same brilliant light which I had seen at the door of the
room on the day of Seraphina's burial, appeared to
me to rest on these shrubs, and dart its rays towards
me. The avenue in which I was happened to
have been Seraphina's favourite walk.

" The recollection of this inspired me with
courage, and I approached the shrubs in the hope

of meeting my sister's shade beneath the trees.' But my hopes being frustrated, I returned to the house with trembling steps.

" I there found many extraordinary circumstances: nobody had thought of supper, which I imagined would have been half over. All the servants were running about in confusion, and were hastening to pack up the clothes and furniture.

" ' Who is going away ?' I demanded.'

" ' Why surely, mademoiselle !' exclaimed the steward, ' are you not acquainted with his excellency's wish to have us all ?'

" ' Wherefore then ?'

" ' This very night we are to set out for his excellency's estate."

" ' Why so ?'

" They shrugged their shoulders. I ran into my father's cabinet, and there found him with his eyes fixed on the ground.

" ' Seraphina's second prophecy is also accomplished,' said he to me, ' though precisely the least likely thing possible.—I am in disgrace.'

" ' What! did she predict this ?'

" ' Yes, my child ; but I concealed it from you. I resign myself to my fate, and leave others better to fill this perilous post. I am about to retire to my own estates, there to live for you, and to constitute the happiness of my vassals.'

" In spite of the violent emotions which were created by my father's misfortune, and the idea of separating from all the friends I loved, his apparent tranquillity produced a salutary effect on my mind. At midnight we set off. My father was so much master of himself under his change of condition, that by the time he arrived at his estate he was calm and serene.

" He found many things to arrange and improve; and his active turn of mind soon led him to find a train of pleasing occupations.

" In a short time, however, he was withdrawn from them, by an illness which the physicians regarded as very serious. My father conformed to all they prescribed : he abstained from all occupation, though he entertained very little hope of any good resulting from it. ' Seraphina,' he said to me (entirely changing his former opinion), 'Seraphina has twice predicted true; and will a third time.'

" This conversation made me very miserable ; for I understood from it that my father believed he should shortly die.

" In fact, he visibly declined, and was at length forced to keep his bed. He one evening sent for me ; and after having dismissed his attendants, he, in a feeble voice, and with frequent interruptions, thus addressed me :—

" ' Experience has cured me of incredulity; When

the clock, strikes nine according to Seraphina's
prediction) I shall be no more. For this reason,
my dear child, I am anxious to address a few
words of advice to you. If possible, remain in
your present state; never marry. Destiny appears to have conspired against our race.——
But no more of this.—To proceed: if ever you
seriously think of marrying, do not, I beseech you,
neglect to read this paper; but my express desire
is, that you do not open it beforehand, as in that
case its contents would cause you unnecessary
misery.'

·: " Saying these words, which with sobbing I
listened to, he drew from under his pillow a sealed
paper, which he gave me. The moment was not
favourable for reflecting on the importance of the
condition which he imposed on me. The clock,
which announced the *fated hour*, at which my father, resting on my shoulder, drew his last gasp,
deprived me of my senses.

·. " The day of his interment was also marked by
the brilliant and extraordinary light of which I
have before made mention.

r " You know, that shortly after this melancholy
loss I returned to the capital, in hopes of finding
consolation in your beloved society. You also know,
that youth seconded your efforts to render existence
desirable; and that by degrees I felt a relish for

life.. Neither are you ignorant that the result
of this intercourse was an attachment between the
count Ernest and me, which rendered my father's
exhortations abortive.. The count loved me, and
I returned his affection, and nothing more was
wanting to make me think that I ought not to lead
a life of celibacy: besides, my father had only
made this request conditionally.

" My marriage appeared certain; and I did not
hesitate to open the mysterious paper. There it is,
I will read it to you :—

" ' Seraphina has undoubtedly already told you,
that when she endeavoured to question the phantom concerning your destiny, it suddenly disappeared. The incomprehensible being seen by your
sister had made mention of you, and its afflicting
decree was, that three days before that fixed on for
your marriage, you would die at the same *ninth*
hour which has been so fatal to us. Your sister re-
covering a little from her first alarm, asked it, if
you could not escape this dreadful mandate by remaining single.

" 'Unhappily, Seraphina did not receive any answer : but I feel assured, that by marrying you
will die. For this reason I entreat you to remain
single : I add, however—if it accords with your inclinations ; as I do not feel confident that even this
will ensure you from the effect of the prediction.

" 'In order, my dear child, to save you from all
premature uneasiness, I have avoided this communication till the hour of danger: reflect, therefore,
seriously on what you ought to do.

" ' My spirit, when you read these lines, shall
hover over and bless you, whatever way you decide.' "

Florentina folded up the paper again in silence; and, after a pause which her two friends
sensibly felt, added:—

" Possibly, my dear friends, this has caused the
change in me which you have sometimes condemned. But tell me whether, situated as I am,
you would not become troubled, and almost annihilated, by the prediction which announced your
death on the very eve of your happiness?

" Here my recital ends. To-morrow the count
returns from his travels. The ardour of his affection has induced him to fix on the third day after
his arrival for the celebration of our marriage." .

" Then 'tis this very day!" exclaimed Amelia and Maria at the same moment; paleness and
inquietude depicted on every feature, when their
eyes glanced to a clock on the point of striking
nine.

" Yes, this is indeed the decisive day," replied
Florentina, with a grave yet serene air. " The

morning has been to me a frightful one; but at
this moment I find myself composed, my health is
excellent, and gives me 'a. confidence ' that death
would with difficulty overcome me to-day. : Besides, a secret but lively presentiment tells me that
this very evening the wish I have so long formed
will be accomplished. My beloved sister will appear to me, and will defeat the 'prediction concerning me.

"Dear Seraphina! you were so suddenly, so
cruelly snatched from me! Where are you, that I
may, return, with tenfold interest, the love that I
have not the power of proving towards you?"

The two sisters, transfixed with horror, had their
eyes riveted on the clock, which struck the *fated*
hour.

"You are welcome!" cried Florentina, seeing
the fire in the chimney, to which they had paid no
attention, suddenly extinguished. She then rose
from her chair; and with open arms walked towards the door which Maria and Amelia anxiously
regarded, whilst sighs escaped them both; and at
which entered the figure of Seraphina, illumined
by the moon's rays. Florentina folded her sister
in her arms.—"I am thine for ever!"

These words, pronounced in a soft and melancholy tone of voice, struck Amelia and Maria's

ears; but they knew not whether they were uttered by Florentina or the phantom, or whether by both the sisters together.

Almost at the same moment the servants came in, alarmed, to learn what had happened. They had heard a noise as if all the glasses and porcelain in the house were breaking. They found their mistress extended at the door, but not the slightest trace of the apparition remained.

Every means of restoring Florentina to life were used, but in vain. The physicians attributed her death to a ruptured blood-vessel. Maria and Amelia will carry the remembrance of this heart-rending scene to their graves.

III.

THE DEATH'S HEAD.

———— " What guilt
Can equal violations of the dead?
The dead how sacred !"————
YOUNG'S NIGHT THOUGHTS.

THE beauty of the evening which succeeded to a very sultry day tempted colonel Kielholm to sit, surrounded by his little family, on the stone bench placed before the door of the noble mansion he had recently purchased. In order to become acquainted by degrees with his new tenants, he took pleasure in questioning on their occupations and conditions the greater part of those who passed by; he alleviated their little sufferings by his advice as well as by his bounty. His family enjoyed particular pleasure in seeing the little inn situated in front of the *château*, which, instead of presenting a disgusting object, as when the late owner lived there, became each succeeding day better and more orderly. Their pleasure was heightened from the circumstance that the new landlord, who had been many

years a servant in the family, was loud in praises of
its amended condition, and delighted himself in his
new calling, with the idea of the happy prospects it
held forth to himself, his wife, and children. : ...

Formerly, though the road was greatly frequented, nobody ventured to pass a night at this
inn; but now each day there was a succession of
travellers; carriages were constantly seen at the
door or in the court-yard; and the air of general
satisfaction of each party as they proceeded on
their route, incontestably proved to the landlord,
(who always, hat in hand, was at the door of their
carriages as they drove off,) that his efforts to give
the various travellers satisfaction were completely
successful.

A moving scene of this nature had just disappeared, which furnished conversation for the
moment, when a whimsical equipage, which arrived from another quarter, attracted the attention
of the colonel and his family. A long carriage,
loaded with trunks and all sorts of luggage, and
drawn by two horses, whose form and colour
presented the most grotesque contrast imaginable,
but which in point of meagreness were an excellent
match, was succeeded by a second long and large
vehicle, which they had, most probably at the expense of the adjacent forest, converted into a travelling thicket. The four steeds which drew it, did.

not in any respect make a better appearance than
the two preceding. But the colonel and his family were still more struck by the individuals who
filled this second carriage: it was a strange med-
ley of children and grown persons, closely wedged
together; but not one of their countenances bore
the slightest mark of similarity of ideas. Discon-
tent, aversion, and hatred, were legible in the face
of each of these sun-burnt strangers. It was not a
family, but a collection of individuals which fear
or necessity kept together without uniting. . .

The colonel's penetrating eye led him to discover thus much, though the distance was considerable. He at length saw descend from the back part
of the carriage a man of better appearance than the
others. At something which he said, the whole
troop turned their eyes towards the inn; they as-
sumed an air of greater content, and appeared a
little better satisfied.

The first carriage had already stopped at the
door of the inn, while the second was passing the
château; and the extremely humble salutations
from the passengers in the latter, seemed to claim
the good-will of the colonel and his family.

The second carriage had scarcely stopped, ere
the troop were out of it, each appearing anxious to
quit those next to whom they had been sitting with
all possible speed. The spruce and agile manner

in which they leapt out of the vehicle, left no doubt
on the mind what their profession was,—they could
be none other than rope-dancers.

The colonel remarked, that "notwithstanding the
humble salutations they had made, he did not think
they would exhibit in these parts; but according to
appearances they would proceed to the capital
with all possible dispatch; as it was hardly to be
expected that they would be delayed a single day,
by the very trivial profit to be expected from ex-
hibiting in a mere country village."

"We have," said he, "seen the worst side of
these gentry, without the probability of ascertain-
ing whether, they have any thing to recommend
them to our notice."

His wife was on the point of expressing her dislike to all those tricks which endanger the neck,
when the person whom they had observed as being superior to the rest, advanced towards them,
and after making a low bow, asked permission to
remain there a few days. The colonel was unable
to refuse this request, as he shewed him a passport
properly signed.

"I beg you," replied the colonel, "to declare
most positively to your company, that every equi-
vocal action is punished in my villages; as I am
anxious to avoid all possibility of quarrels."

"Do not in the least alarm yourself, Monsieur;

H

an extremely severe discipline is kept up in my troop, which has in some respects the effect of a secret police among ourselves: all can answer for one, and one can answer for all. Each is bound to communicate any misconduct on the part of another to me, and is always rewarded for such communication; but, on the contrary, if he omits so to do, he is severely punished,"

The colonel's lady could not conceal her aversion to such a barbarous regulation; which the stranger perceiving, shrugged his shoulders. "We must all accommodate our ideas to our condition. I have found, that if persons of this stamp are not so treated, there is no possibility of governing them. And you may the more confidently rely on my vigilance, as I had the happiness of being born in this place, and in consequence feel a double obligation: first, to the place of my birth; secondly, to his worship."

"Were you born here?" demanded the colonel's wife, with surprise.

"Yes, my lady; my father was Schurster the schoolmaster, who died lately. But I call myself Calzolaro, finding that my profession succeeds better under an Italian than a German name."

This explanation redoubled the interest the colonel and his lady already felt for this man, who appeared to have received a tolerable education.

They knew that the schoolmaster, whose profession had been pretty lucrative, owing to the numerous population of the village, had died worth some considerable property; but that he had named a distant female relation as his sole heiress, leaving his only son an extremely scanty pittance.

"My father," continued Calzolaro, "did not behave to me as he ought: and I cannot but think I should be justified in availing myself of some important informalities in his will; and endeavouring to set it aside, which is my present intention. But excuse, I pray you, my having tired your patience with relations to which the conversation has involuntarily given rise. I have still one more request to make: Permit me to return you my best thanks for your gracious condescension, and to shew you some of the exercises for which my troop is famous."

The colonel acceded to Calzolaro's request, and a day was fixed for the performance.

Calzolaro went that very evening to the village pastor, and communicated to him his intentions relative to his father's will. The worthy minister condemned such procedure, and endeavoured to convince Calzolaro that his father's anger was just. "Picture to yourself, young man," said he, "a father who has grown old in an honest profession, and who rejoices in having a son to whom he can leave it: added to which, this son has great talents, a good

H 2

understanding, and is well-disposed. It was natural
that the father should use every possible exertion to
obtain for this son his own situation at his death.
The son is in truth nominated to succeed him. The
father, thinking himself secure from misfortune,
feels quite happy. It was at this period that the
son, enticed by hair-brained companions, gave up
a certain and respectable, though not very brilliant
provision. My dear Schurster, if, when shaking off
the salutary yoke, and quitting your venerable father, to ramble over the world, you could lightly
forget the misery it would occasion him, you ought
at least in the present instance, to behave differ-
ently; or, in plain terms, I shall say you are a
good-for-nothing fellow. Did not your father,
even after this, do all he could to reclaim you? but
you were deaf to his remonstrances."

" Because the connexion which I had formed
imposed obligations on me, from which I could
not free myself, as from a garment of which one is
tired. For had I then been my own master, as I
now am ——"

" Here let us stop, if you please : I have only
one request to make of you. You ought, from respect to your father's memory, not to dispute his
will."

This conversation and the venerable air of the
pastor had a little shaken Calzolaro's resolutions :

but the next day they returned with double force;
for he heard several persons say, that shortly before his death, his father was heard to speak of him
with great bitterness.   :

This discourse rendered him so indignant, that
he would not even accede to a proposal of accommodation with the heiress, made to him by the
pastor.

The colonel tried equally, but without success,
to become a mediator, and at length determined to
let the matter take its course.

He however assisted at the rehearsals made by
the troop; and took so much pleasure in the per-
formances prepared for the amusement of him and
his family by Calzolaro, that he engaged him to
act again, and invited several of his neighbours to
witness them.

Calzolaro said to him on this occasion: "You
have as yet seen very trifling proofs of our abilities.
But do not fancy that I am an idle spectator, and
merely stand by to criticize :—I, as well as each individual of my troop, have a sphere of action; and
I reserve myself to give you, before we take our
leave, some entertaining experiments in electricity
and magnetism."

The colonel then told him, that he had recently
seen in the capital a man who exhibited experiments of that sort, which had greatly delighted him;

and above all, he had been singularly astonished
by his powers of ventriloquism. :

" It is precisely in that particular point," replied
Calzolaro, that I think myself equal to any one,
be they whom they may." . . . . .

" I am very glad of it," answered the colonel.
" But what would produce the most astonishing
effect on those who have never heard a ventriloquist, would be a dialogue between the actor and
a death's head :—the man of whom I made mention
gave us one."

" If you command it, I can undertake it." .

" Delightful!" exclaimed the colonel. And
Calzolaro having given some unequivocal proofs
of his powers as a ventriloquist, the colonel added : " The horror of the scene must be augmented
by every possible means : for instance, we must
hang the room with black ; the lights must be extinguished ; we must fix on midnight. It will be
a species of phantasmagoria dessert after supper ;
an unexpected spectacle. We must contrive to
throw the audience into a cold perspiration, in order that when the explanation takes place they
may have ample reason to laugh at their fears.
For if all succeeds, no one will be exempt from a
certain degree of terror."

Calzolaro entered into the project, and promised that nothing should be neglected to make it

successful.—They unfurnished a closet, and hung it
with black.

The colonel's wife was the only one admitted to
their confidence, as they could rely on her discretion. Her husband had even a little altercation
on the subject with her. She wished, that for the
ventriloquist scene they should use the model of a
head in plaister, which her son used to draw from;
whereas the colonel maintained that they must have
a real skull : " Otherwise," said he, " the spectators' illusion will speedily be at an end; but after
they have heard the death's head speak, we will
cause it to be handed round, in order to convince
them that it is in truth but a skull."

—" And where can we procure this skull ?" asked
the colonel's wife.

" The sexton will undertake to provide us with
it."

" And whose corpse will you thus disturb, for a
frivolous amusement ?"

" How sentimental you are!" replied Kielholm,
who did not consider the subject in so serious a
light : " We may easily see you are not accustomed
to the field of battle, where no further respect is
paid to the repose of the dead, than suits the con-
venience of the labourer in the fields where they are
buried."

" God preserve me from such a spectacle!" ex-

claimed the colonel's lady in quitting them, when
she perceived her husband was insensible to her representations.

According to the orders which he received, the
sexton one night brought a skull in good preservation.

The morning of the day destined for the representation, Calzolaro went into the adjacent forest
to rehearse the dialogue which he was to have with
the death's head. He considered in what way to
place the head, so as to avoid all suspicion of the
answers given by it being uttered by a person concealed. In the mean while the pastor arrived at
the spot from a neighbouring hamlet, where he
had been called to attend a dying person : and be-
lieving that the interposition of Providence was visible in this accidental meeting, the good man
stopped, in order once again to exhort Calzolaro
to agree to an accommodation with the heiress.

" I yesterday," said he, " received a letter from
her, in which she declares that, rather than any dis-
respect should be paid to your father's last will and
testament, she will give up to you half the inheritance to which she is thereby entitled. Ought you
not to prefer this to a process at law, the issue of
which is doubtful, and which at all events will never do you credit ?"

Calzolaro persisted in declaring that the law

should decide between him and the testator.—The
poor young man was not in a state to see in a proper point of view his father's conduct towards
him.—The pastor, finding all his representations
and entreaties fruitless, left him. Calzolaro proceeded slowly to the inn, to assign to each of his
band their particular part. .. He told them that he
should not be with them ; but notwithstanding he
should have an eye over their conduct. He was
not willing to appear, as the manager of these
mountebanks, to the party assembled at the colonel's, thinking that if he appeared for the first time
in the midnight scene, as an entire stranger, it
would add still more to the marvellous.

The tumblers' tricks and rope-dancing were performed to admiration. And those of the spectators whose constant residence in the country prevented their having witnessed similar feats, were
the most inclined to admire and praise the agility
of the troop. The little children in particular were
applauded. The compassion excited by their unhappy destiny, mingled with the approbation bestowed on them ; and the ladies were subjects of
envy, in giving birth to the satisfaction depicted in
the countenances of these little wretches by their
liberal donations.

The agility of the troop formed the subject of
general conversation the whole afternoon. They

were even speaking in their praise after supper,—
when the master of the house said to the company
assembled:

" I am rejoiced, my dear friends, to see the
pleasure you have received from the little spectacle
that I have been enabled to give you. My joy is
so much the greater, since I find you doubting the
possibility of things which are very natural; for I
have it in my power to submit for your examination something of a very incomprehensible nature.
At this very moment I have in my house a person
who entertains a most singular intercourse with the
world of spirits, and who can compel the dead to
answer his questions."

" O!" exclaimed a lady smiling, " don't terrify
us."

" You jest *now*," replied the colonel; " but I
venture to affirm your mirth will be a little
changed when the scene takes place."

" I accept the challenge," answered the incredulous fair one. All the party was of her opinion,
and declared themselves so openly and so loudly
against the truth of these terrific scenes, that the
colonel began to be really apprehensive for the
effects likely to be produced by those he had prepared. He would have even relinquished his project, if his guests, one and all, had not intreated him
to the contrary. They even went further: they be-

sought him not long to delay the wonderful things
he promised. But the colonel, keeping his own
counsel, feigned ignorance that they were laughing
at him; and with a grave air declared that the ex-
periment could not take place till midnight.   ⸳
⸳. The clock at length struck twelve. ., The colonel gave his servants orders to place chairs facing
the door of a closet which had been hitherto kept
shut: he invited the company to sit down, and
gave orders for all the lights to be put out. While
these preparations were making, he thus addressed
the company: . ;   . ⸳: . . . ...,   ⸳   ⸳
⸳ ⸳" I entreat you, my friends, to abstain from all
idle curiosity."... The grave and solemn tone in
which he uttered these words made a deep impression on the party, whose incredulity was not a
little lessened by the striking of the clock, and the
putting out the lights one after the other.   Presently they heard from the closet facing them the
hoarse and singular sounds by which it is pretended spirits are conjured up ; and which were
interrupted at intervals by loud strokes of a ham-
mer. All on a sudden the door of the closet
opened: and as by slow degrees the cloud of incense which filled it evaporated, they gradually discovered the black trappings with which it was
hung, and an altar in the middle also hung with
black drapery. On this altar was placed a skull,

which cast its terrifying regards on all the company present.

Meanwhile the spectators' breathing became more audible and difficult, and their embarrassment increased in proportion as the vapour gave place to a brilliant light issuing from an alabaster lamp suspended from the cieling. Many of them indeed turned their heads away in alarm on hearing a noise behind them; which, however, they discovered simply proceeded from some of the servants, whom the colonel had given permission to be present during the exhibition, at a respectful distance.

After a moment of profound silence, Calzolaro entered. A long beard had so effectually altered his youthful appearance, that though several of the spectators had previously seen him, they could not possibly recognize him under this disguise. And his Oriental costume added so much to the deceit, that his entrance had an excellent effect.

In order that his art should impose the more, the colonel recommended to him a degree of haughtiness in addressing the company; and that he should not salute them according to any prescribed forms of politeness, but to announce himself in terms foreign from all ordinary modes of conversation. They both agreed that a mysterious jargon would best answer their purpose.

In consequence of such determination, Calzo-

laro, assuming a deep sepulchral tone, thus began:
—" After our present state of existence, we are
swallowed up in the obscure abyss which we call
death,' in order that we may become incorporated
in an entirely new and peaceful state. It is in order to emancipate the soul from this state, that the
sublime 'arts are exercised; and to create among
fools and weak persons the idea of its being impossible! The wise and learned pity them for their
ignorance, in not knowing what is possible and
impossible, true or false, light or dark; because
they do not know and cannot comprehend the exalted spirits, who, from the silence of the vault
and the grave, from the mouldering bones of the
dead, speak to the living in a voice no less formidable than true. As to you, who are now here
assembled, listen to a word of advice: Avoid pro-
voking by any indiscreet question the vengeance of
the spirit, who at my command will be invisibly
stationed beneath this human skull. Endeavour to
moderate your fear: listen to every thing with
calmness and submission; for I take under my
especial care all those who are obedient, and only
leave the guilty as a prey to the destruction they
merit."

The colonel remarked with secret satisfaction
the impression produced on the company, hitherto
so incredulous, by this pompous harangue.

" Every thing succeeds better than I could have
hoped," said he, in an under tone to his wife, who
was not at all amused by the performance, and
who was only present to please her husband.

- Meanwhile Calzolaro continued: " Look on
this pitiful and neglected head : my magic art has
removed the bolts of the tomb to which it was
consigned, and in which reposes a long line of
princes.' The owner of it is now actually there;
rendering up to the spirits an exact account of the
life he had led. Don't be alarmed, even though
it should burst forth in terrible menaces against
you: and against me his impotency will be manifest,
as, spite of his former grandeur, he cannot resist the
power I have over him, provided no culpable pre-
cipitation on your part interrupt the solemnity of
my questions."

. He then opened a door of the closet hitherto
concealed from the company, brought a chafing-
dish filled with red-hot coals, threw thereon some
incense, and walked three times round the altar;
pronouncing at each circle a spell. He then drew
from its scabbard a sword which hung in his girdle,
plunged it in the smoke issuing from the incense,
and making frightful contortions of his face and
limbs, pretended to endeavour to cleave the head,
which, however, he did not touch. At last he took
the head up on the point of his sword, held it up

in th e air before him, and advanced towards the spectators a little moved.

"Who art thou, miserable dust, that I hold at the point of my sword ?" demanded Calzolaro with a confident air and a firm voice.—But scarcely had he uttered this question, when he turned pale ; his arm trembled ; his knees shook ; his haggard eyes, which were fixed on the head, were horror-struck : he had hardly strength sufficient to place the head and the sword on the altar, ere he suddenly fell on the floor with every symptom of extreme terror. The spectators, frightened out of their wits, looked at the master of the house, who in his turn looked at them. No one seemed to know whether this was to be considered part of the scene, nor whether it was possible to explain it. The curiosity of the audience was raised to its utmost pitch: they waited still a considerable time, but no explanation took place. At length Calzolaro, half-raising himself, asked if his father's shadow had disappeared.

Stupefaction succeeded astonishment. The colonel was anxious to know whether he was still attempting to impose on the company by a pretended dialogue with the death's head ?

Calzolaro answered that he would do any thing, and that he would willingly submit to any punishment they chose to inflict on him for his frightful crime: but he entreated they would instantly carry back the head to its place of repose. His countenance had undergone a complete change, and only resumed its wonted appearance on the colonel's wife acquiescing in his wish: she ordered the head to be instantly conveyed to the church-yard, and to be replaced in the grave.

During this unexpected denouement, every eye was turned on Calzolaro; he, who not long ago was talking with so much emphasis and in such a lofty strain, could now scarcely draw his breath; and from time to time threw supplicating looks on the spectators, as if entreating them to wait patiently till he had recovered strength sufficient to continue his performance.

The colonel informed them in the mean while of the species of jest that he had projected to play on them, and for the failure of which he could not at that moment account. At last Calzolaro, with an abashed air, spoke as follows:—

" The spectacle which I designed to have given, has terminated in a terrible manner for me. But, happily for the honourable company present, I perceive they did not see the frightful apparition which caused me a temporary privation of my reason. Scarcely had I raised the death's head on the point of my sword, and had begun to address it, than it appeared to me in my father's features:

and whether my, ears, deceived me or not, I am
ignorant; neither do I know how I was restored
to my senses; but I heard it say, 'Tremble, parri-
cide, whom nothing can convert, and who wilt not,
turn to the path thou hast abandoned!' ".

..The very recollection produced such horror on
Calzolaro's mind as to stop his respiration and
prevent his proceeding. . The colonel briefly explained to the spectators what appeared to them
mysterious in his words, and then said to the peni-
tent juggler:

"Since your imagination has played you so
strange a trick, I exhort you in future to avoid all
similar accidents, and to accept the arrangement
proposed to you by the person whom your father
has named as his heir."

" No, monsieur," answered he, " no agreement,
no bargain; else I shall only half fulfil my duty.
Every thing shall belong to this heiress, and the
law-suit shall be abandoned."

He at the same time declared that he was
weary of the mode of life he had adopted, and that
every wish of his father's should be fulfilled.

. The colonel told him that such a resolution
compensated for what had failed in the evening's
amusement.

The company, however, did not cease making
numberless inquiries of Calzolaro, many of which

were very ludicrous. They were anxious to know, among other things, whether the head which had appeared to him, resembled that of a corpse or a living being.

" It most probably belongs to a corpse," he replied. " I was so thunderstruck with the horrible effect of it, that I cannot remember minutiæ. Imagine an only son, with the point of a sword which he holds in his hand, piercing his father's skull ! The bare idea is sufficient to deprive one of one's senses."

" I did not believe," answered the colonel, after having for some time considered Calzolaro, " that the conscience of a man, who like you has rambled the world over, could still be so much overcome by the powers of imagination."

" What! monsieur, do you still doubt the reality of the apparition, though I am ready to attest it by the most sacred oaths ?"

" Your assertion contradicts itself. We have also our eyes to see what really exists; and nobody, excepting yourself, saw any other than a simple skull."

" That is what I cannot explain : but this I can add, that I am firmly persuaded, although even now I cannot account for my so thinking, that as sure as I exist, that head is actually and truly the head of my father : I am ready to attest it by my most solemn oath."

"To prevent your perjuring yourself, they shall instantly go to the sexton, and learn the truth."
Saying this, the colonel went out to give the necessary orders. He returned an instant afterwards, saying :—

" Here is another strange phænomenon. The sexton is in this house; but is not able to answer my questions. Anxious to enjoy the spectacle I was giving my friends; he mixed with some of my servants, who, possessing the same degree of curiosity, had softly opened the door through which the chaffing-dish was conveyed. But at the moment of the conjurer falling on the floor, the same insensibility overcame the sexton; who even now has not recovered his reason, although they have used every possible method to restore him."

One of the party said, that, being subject to fainting himself, he constantly carried about him a liquor, the effect of which was wonderful in such cases, and that he would go and try it now on the sexton. They all followed him: but this did not succeed better than the methods previously resorted to.

" This man must indeed be dead," said the person who had used the liquor without effect on him.

The clock in the tower had just struck one, and every person thought of retiring; but slight symptoms of returning life being perceptible in the sexton, they still remained.

"God be praised!" exclaimed the sexton awaking; "he is at length restored to rest!"

"Who, old dad?" said the colonel.

"Our late schoolmaster."

"What then, that head was actually his?"

"Alas! if you will only promise not to be angry with me, I will confess——It was his."

The colonel then asked him how the idea of disturbing the schoolmaster's corpse in particular came into his head.

"Owing to a diabolical boldness. It is commonly believed, that when a child speaks to the head of its deceased parent at the midnight hour, the head comes to life again. I was anxious to prove the fact, but shall never recover from its effects: happily, however, the head is actually restored to rest."

They asked him how he knew it. He answered, that he had seen it all the while he was in a state of lethargy; that as the clock struck one, his wife had finished re-interring the head in its grave. And he described in the most minute manner how she held it.

The curiosity of the company assembled was so much excited by witnessing these inexplicable events, that they awaited the return of the servant whom the colonel had dispatched to the sexton's wife. Every thing had happened precisely as he described;—the clock struck one at the very moment the head was laid in the grave.

. These events had produced to the spectators a night of much greater terrors than the colonel had prepared for them. Nay, even *his* imagination was raised to such a pitch, that the least breath of wind, or the slightest noise, appeared to him as a forerunner to some disagreeable visitor from the world of spirits.

He was out of his bed at dawn of day, to look out of his window and see the occasion of the noise which at that hour was heard at the inn-door. He saw the rope-dancers seated in the carriage, about to take their departure. Calzolaro was not with them; but presently afterwards came to the side of the vehicle, where he took leave of them: the children seemed to leave him behind with regret.

The carriage drove off; and the colonel made a signal to Calzolaro to come and speak to him.

"I apprehend," said he to him, when he came in, "that you have taken entire leave of your troop."

"Well, monsieur, ought I not so to do?"

"It appears to me a procedure in which you have acted with as little reflection as the one

which tempted you first to join them. You ought
rather to have availed yourself of some favourable
occasion for withdrawing the little capital that you
have in their funds."

"Do you then, monsieur colonel, forget what
has happened to me; and that I could not have enjoyed another moment of repose in the society of
persons who are only externally men? Every time
I recall the scene of last night to my recollection,
my very blood freezes in my veins. From this moment I must do all in my power to appease my
father's shade, which is now so justly incensed
against me. Without much effort I have withdrawn myself from a profession which never had
any great charms for me. Reflect only on the
misery of being the chief of a troop, who, to earn
a scanty morsel of bread, are compelled every moment to risk their lives !—and even this morsel of
bread not always attainable. Moreover, I know
that the clown belonging to the troop, who is a
man devoid of all sentiment, has for a long while
aspired to become the chief : and I know that he
has for some time been devising various means to
remove me from this world ; therefore it appears
to me that I have not been precipitate in relin-
quishing my rights to him for a trifling sum of
money. I only feel for the poor children ; and
would willingly have purchased them, to save them

from so unhappy a career; but he would not take
any price for them. I have only one consolation,
which is, the hope that the inhuman treatment they
will experience at his hands will induce them to
make their escape, and follow a better course of
life."

· " And what do you purpose doing yourself ?"
·. " I have told you, that I shall retire to some
obscure corner of Germany, and follow the profession to which my father destined me."

., The colonel made him promise to wait a little;
and, if possible, he would do something for him.

, In the interim, the heiress to his father's property arrived, to have a conference on the subject
with him. As soon as he had made known his intentions to her, she entreated him no longer to refuse half the inheritance, or at least to receive it as
a voluntary gift on her part. The goodness, the
sweetness of this young person, (who was pretty
also,) so pleased Calzolaro, that a short time afterwards he asked her hand in marriage. She consented to give it to him. And the colonel then
exerted himself more readily in behalf of this man,
who had already gained his favour. He fulfilled
his wishes, by sending him to a little property belonging to his wife, to follow the profession his
father had fixed on for him.

Ere he set off, Calzolaro resumed his German

name of Schurster. The good pastor, who had so
recently felt indignant at his obstinacy, gave the
nuptial benediction· to the happy couple in presence of the colonel and his family, who on this
occasion gave an elegant entertainment at the
château.

In the evening, a little after sun-set, the bride
and bridegroom were walking in the garden, at
some little distance from the rest of the company,
and appeared plunged in a deep reverie. All
on a sudden they looked at each other ; for it
seemed to them, that some one took a hand of
each and united them. They declared, at· least,
that the idea of this action having taken place
came to them both so instantaneously and so involuntarily, that they were astonished at it themselves. ·

An instant afterwards, they distinctly heard these
words :—

" May God bless your union !". pronounced by
the voice of Calzolaro's father.

. The bridegroom told the colonel, some time afterwards, that without these consolatory words, the
terrible apparition which he saw on the memorable
night, would assuredly have haunted him all his
life, and have impoisoned his happiest moments. ·

IV.

THE DEATH-BRIDE.

———— " She shall be such
As walk'd your first queen's ghost————".
SHAKSPEARE.

THE summer had been uncommonly fine, and the
baths crowded with company beyond all comparison: but still the public rooms were scarce ever filled, and never gay. The nobility and military asso-
ciated only with those of their own rank, and the
citizens contented themselves by slandering both
parties. So many partial divisions necessarily
proved an obstacle to a general and united assembly.

Even the public balls did not draw the *beau-
monde* together, because the proprietor of the
baths appeared there bedizened with insignia of
knighthood; and this glitter, added to the stiff
manners of this great man's family, and the tribe
of lackeys in splendid liveries who constantly attended him, compelled the greater part of the com-

pany assembled, silently to observe the rules prescribed to them according to their different ranks.

For these reasons the balls became gradually
less numerously attended. Private parties were
formed, in which it was endeavoured·to preserve
the charms that were daily diminishing in the public assemblies.

One of these: societies met. generally ·twice a
week in a room which at that time ·was usually
unoccupied. There they supped, and afterwards
enjoyed, either in a walk abroad, or remaining in
the room, the charms of unrestrained conversation.
· .The members of·.this· society were already acquainted, at least by name ; but an Italian marquis,
who had lately joined their party, was unknown to
them; and indeed to every one assembled at the
baths. · ·

. The title of *Italian* marquis appeared the more·
singular, as his name, according to the entry of it
in the general list, seemed·to denote him of Northern extraction, and was composed of so great a
number of consonants, that no one could pronounce it without difficulty.

·His physiognomy and ·manners likewise presented many singularities. His long and wan visage,
his black eyes, his imperious look, had so little of
attraction in them, that every one would certainly
have avoided him, had he not possessed a fund of

entertaining stories, the relation of which proved
an excellent antidote to *ennui*: the only draw-
back against them was, that in general they required rather too great a share of credulity on the
part of his auditors.

The party had one day just risen from table,
and found themselves but ill inclined for gaiety.
They were still too much fatigued from the ball of
the preceding evening to enjoy the recreation of
walking, although invited so to do by the bright
light of the moon. They were even unable to
keep up any conversation; therefore it is not to be
wondered at, that they were more than usually
anxious for the marquis to arrive.

" Where can he be?" exclaimed the countess
in an impatient tone.

" Doubtless still at the faro-table, to the no
small grief of the bankers," replied Florentine.
" This very morning he has occasioned the sudden
departure of two of these gentlemen."

" No great loss," answered another.

" To us——," replied Florentine; " but it is to
the proprietor of the baths, who only prohibited
gambling, that it might be pursued with greater
avidity."

" The marquis ought to abstain from such
achievements," said the chevalier with an air of
mystery. " Gamblers are revengeful, and have ge-

nerally advantageous connections. If what is whispered be correct, that the marquis is unfortunately
implicated in political affairs——."

" But," demanded the countess, "what then has
the marquis done to the bankers of the gaming-
table ?"   ,   ;

. " Nothing ; except that he betted on cards
which almost invariably won. And what renders
it rather singular, he scarcely derived any advantage from it himself, for he always adhered to the
weakest party. But the other punters were not so
scrupulous ; for they charged their cards in such a
manner that the bank broke before the deal had
gone round."

The countess was on the point of asking other
questions, when the marquis coming in changed
the conversation.

. . " Here you are at last !" exclaimed several persons at the same moment.

" We have," said the countess, " been most
anxious for your society ; and just on this day you
have been longer than usual absent."

. " I have projected an important expedition ; and
it has succeeded to my wishes. I hope by to-
morrow there will not be a single gaming-table
left here. I have been from one gambling-room
to another ; and there are not sufficient post-horses
to carry off the ruined bankers."

- "And cannot you," asked the countess, "teach us your wonderful art of always winning?" ·

"It would be a difficult task, my fair lady; and in order to do it, one must ensure a fortunate hand, for without that nothing could be done."

: "Nay," replied the chevalier, laughing, "never did I see so fortunate an one as yours."

"As you are still very young, my dear chevalier, you have many novelties to witness."

Saying these words, the marquis threw on the chevalier so piercing a look that the latter cried:

"Will you then cast my nativity?"

"Provided that it is not done to-day," said the countess; "for who knows whether your future destiny will afford us so amusing a history as that which the marquis two days since promised we should enjoy?"

"I did not exactly say amusing."

"But at least full of extraordinary events: and we require some such, to draw us from the lethargy which has overwhelmed us all day."

"Most willingly: but first I am anxious to learn whether any of you know aught of the surprising things related of the Death-Bride."

No one remembered to have heard speak of her.

The marquis appeared anxious to add something more by way of preface; but the countess and the rest of the party so openly manifested their impatience, that the marquis began his narration as follows:—

" I had for a long time projected a visit to the count Lieppa, at his estates in Bohemia. We had met each other in almost every country in Europe: attracted *hither* by the frivolity of youth to partake of every pleasure which presented itself, but led *thither* when years of discretion had rendered us more sedate and steady.—At length, in our more advanced age, we ardently desired, ere the close of life, once again to enjoy, by the charms of recollection, the moments of delight which we had passed together. For my part, I was anxious to see the castle of my friend, which was, according to his description, in an extremely romantic district. It was built some hundred years back by his ancestors; and their successors had preserved it with so much care, that it still maintained its imposing appearance, at the same time it afforded a comfortable abode. The count generally passed the greater part of the year at it with his family, and only returned to the capital at the approach of winter. Being well acquainted with his movements, I did not think it needful to announce my visit; and I arrived at the castle one evening precisely at the time when I knew he would be there; and as I approached it, could not but admire the

variety and beauty of · the 'scenery .which. surrounded it. _ · · · : , . . : : . . · : , : .

  " The hearty welcome which · I received .could
not, however, entirely conceal from my observation
the secret grief depicted on the countenances of the
count, his .wife, ·and their daughter, the lovely Ida.
In a short time I discovered that they still mourned
the loss of Ida's twin-sister,, who had died about a
year .before.) Ida and Hildegarde resembled each
other so much,· that: they were only to be distinguished 'from each . other by. a slight mark of a
strawberry visible on ! Hildegarde's. neck. . Her
room, and every thing in it, was left precisely in the
same state as when she was alive, and the family
were in the habit of visiting it whenever they wished
to indulge the sad satisfaction of meditating on the
loss of this beloved child. The two sisters had but
one heart, one mind : and the parents could not but
apprehend that their separation would be but of
short duration; they dreaded lest Ida should also
be taken from them. , · · '. '. ·

  " I did every thing in my power to amuse this
excellent family, by entertaining them with laugh-
able anecdotes of my younger days, and by directing
their thoughts to less melancholy subjects than
that which now wholly occupied them. I had the
satisfaction of discovering that my efforts were not
ineffectual.' Sometimes we walked in the canton-

round the castle, which was decked with all the
beauties of summer; at other times we took a survey of the different apartments of the castle, and
were astonished at their wonderful state of preservation, whilst we amused ourselves by talking
over the actions of the past generation, whose portraits hung in a long gallery.

"One evening the count had been speaking to
me in confidence, on the subject of his future
plans: among other subjects he expressed his
anxiety, that Ida (who had already, though only in
her sixteenth year, refused several offers) should
be happily married; when suddenly the gardener,
quite out of breath, came to tell us he had seen the
ghost (as he believed, the old chaplain belonging
to the castle), who had appeared a century back.
Several of the servants followed the gardener, and
their pallid countenances confirmed the alarming
tidings he had brought.

"'I believe you will shortly be afraid of your
own shadow,' said the count to them. He then
sent them off, desiring them not again to trouble
him with the like fooleries.

"'It is really terrible,' said he to me, 'to see to
what lengths superstition will carry persons of
that rank of life; and it is impossible wholly to un-
deceive them. From one generation to another an
absurd report has from time to time been spread

abroad, of an old chaplain's ghost wandering in the environs of the castle; and that he says mass in the chapel, with other idle stories of a similar nature. This report has greatly died away since I came into possession of the castle; but it now appears to me, it will never be altogether forgotten.'

" At this moment the duke de Marino was announced. The count did not recollect ever having heard of him.

" I told him that I was tolerably well acquainted with his family; and that I had lately been present, in Venice, at the betrothing of a young man of that name.

" The very same young man came in while I was speaking. I should have felt very glad at seeing him, had I not perceived that my presence caused him evident uneasiness.

" ' Ah,' said he in a tolerably gay tone, after the customary forms of politeness had passed between us; ' the finding you here, my dear marquis, explains to me an occurrence, which with shame I own caused me a sensation of fear. To my no small surprise, they knew my name in the adjacent district; and as I came up the hill which leads to the castle, I heard it pronounced three times in a voice wholly unknown to me: and in a still more audible tone this strange voice bade me welcome. I now, however, conclude it was yours.'

K

" I assured him, (and with truth,) that till his name was announced the minute before, I was ignorant of his arrival, and that none of my servants knew him; for that the valet who accompanied me into Italy was not now with me.

" 'And above all,' added I, ' it would be impossible to discover any equipage, however well known to one, in so dark an evening.'

" ' That is what astonishes me,' exclaimed the duke, a little amazed.

" The incredulous count very politely added, ' that the voice which had told the duke he was welcome, had at least expressed the sentiments of all the family.'

" Marino, ere he said a word relative to the motive of his visit, asked a private audience of me; and confided in me, by telling me that he was come with the intention of obtaining the lovely Ida's hand; and that if he was able to procure her consent, he should demand her of her father.

" ' The countess Apollonia, your bride elect, is then no longer living?' asked I.

" ' We will talk on that subject hereafter,' answered he.

" The deep sigh which accompanied these words led me to conclude that Apollonia had been guilty of infidelity or some other crime towards the duke ; and consequently I thought that

I ought to abstain from any further questions, which appeared to rend his heart, already so sensibly wounded.

"Yet, as he begged me to become his mediator with the count, in order to obtain from him his consent to the match, I painted in glowing colours the danger of an alliance, which he had no other motive for contracting, than the wish to obliterate the remembrance of a dearly, and without doubt, still more tenderly, beloved object. But he assured me that he was far from thinking of the lovely Ida from so blameable a motive, and that he should be the happiest of men if she but proved propitious to his wishes.

" His expressive and penetrating tone of voice, while he said this, lulled the uneasiness that I was beginning to feel; and I promised him I would prepare the count Lieppa to listen to his entreaties, and would give him the necessary information relative to the fortune and family of Marino. But I declared to him at the same time, that I should by no means hurry the conclusion of the affair by my advice, as I was not in the habit of taking upon myself so great a charge as the uncertain issue of a marriage.

" The duke signified his satisfaction at what I said, and made me give (what then appeared to me of no consequence) a promise, that I would not

make mention of the former marriage he was on
the point of contracting, as it would necessarily
bring on a train of unpleasant explanations.

"The duke's views succeeded with a promptitude
beyond his most sanguine hopes. His well-pro-
portioned form, and sparkling eyes smoothed the
paths of love, and introduced him to the heart of
Ida. His agreeable conversation promised to the
mother an amiable son-in-law; and the knowledge
in rural economy, which he evinced as occasions offered, made the count hope for an useful helpmate
in his usual occupations; for since the first day of
the duke's arrival, he had been prevented from
pursuing them.

"Marino followed up these advantages with
great ardour; and I was one evening, much surprised by the intelligence of his being betrothed,
as I did not dream of matters drawing so near a
conclusion. They spoke at table of some bridal
preparations of which I had made mention just
before the duke's arrival at the castle; and the
countess asked me whether that young Marino
was a near relation of the one who was that very
day betrothed to her daughter.'

"'Near enough,' I answered, recollecting my
promise.—Marino looked at me with an air of embarrassment.

"'But, my dear duke,' continued I, 'tell me

who mentioned the amiable Ida to you; or was it
a portrait, or what else, which caused you to think
of looking for a beauty, the selection of whom
does so much honour to your taste, in this remote
corner; for, if I am not mistaken, you said but
yesterday that you had purposed travelling about for
another six months; when all at once (I believe
while in Paris) you changed your plan, and projected a journey wholly and solely to see the
charming Ida?' --

" ' Yes, it was at Paris,' replied the duke ; ' you
are very rightly informed. 1 went there to see and
admire the superb gallery of pictures at the Museum ; but 1 had scarcely entered it, when my eyes
turned from the inanimate beauties, and were riveted on a lady whose incomparable features were
heightened by an air of melancholy. With fear
and trembling I approached her, and only ventured
to follow without speaking to her. I still followed
her after she quitted the gallery; and I drew her
servant aside to learn the name of his mistress. He
told it me : but when I expressed a wish to become acquainted with the father of this beauty, he
said that was next to impossible while at Paris, as
the family were on the point of quitting that city;
nay, of quitting France altogether.

" ' Possibly, however,' said I, ' some opportunity
may present itself.' And I looked every where for

the lady : but she, probably imagining that her servant was following her closely, had continued to
walk on, and was entirely out of sight. . While I
was looking around for her, the servant had likewise vanished from my view.'

"' Who was this beautiful lady ?' asked Ida, in a
tone of astonishment.

"' What! you really did not then perceive me
in the gallery ?'

"' Me!'——' My daughter——!' exclaimed at
the same moment Ida and her parents. ,

. "' Yes, you yourself, mademoiselle. . The servant, whom fortunately for me you left at Paris,
and whom I met the same evening unexpectedly,
as my guardian angel, informed me of all; so that
after a short rest at home, I was able to come
straight hither.'

"' What a fable !' said the count to his daughter, who was mute with astonishment.

. "' Ida,' he added, turning to me, ' has never yet
been out of her native country ; and for myself, I
have not been in Paris these seventeen years.'

. " The duke looked at the count and his daughter
with similar marks of astonishment visible in their
countenances; and conversation would have been
entirely at an end, if I had not taken care to intro-
duce other topics : but I had it nearly all to
myself.

"The repast was no sooner over, than the count took the duke into the recess of a window; and although I was at a considerable distance, and appeared wholly to fix my attention on a new chandelier, I overheard all their conversation.

"' What motive,' demanded the count with a serious and dissatisfied air, 'could have induced you to invent that singular scene in the gallery of the Museum at Paris? for according to my judgment, it could in no way benefit you. Since you are anxious to conceal the cause which brought you to ask my daughter in marriage, at least you might have plainly said as much; and though possibly you might have felt repugnance at making such a declaration, there were a thousand ways of framing your answer, without its being needful thus to offend probability.'

"' Monsieur le comte,' replied the duke much piqued; 'I held my peace at table, thinking that possibly you had reasons for wishing to keep secret your and your daughter's journey to Paris. I was silent merely from motives of discretion; but the singularity of your reproaches compels me to maintain what I have said; and, notwithstanding your reluctance to believe the truth, to declare before all the world, that the capital of France was the spot where I first saw your daughter Ida.'

"' But what if I prove to you, not only by the

witness of my servants, but also by that of all my
tenants, that my daughter has never quitted her na
tive place ?'—

"'I shall still believe the evidence of my own
eyes and ears, which have as great authority over
me.'

"'What you say is really enigmatical,' answered
the count in a graver tone : 'your serious manner convinces me you have been the dupe of some
illusion ; and that you have seen some other person,
whom you have taken for my daughter. Excuse me,
therefore, for having taken up the thing so warmly.'

"'Another person! What then, I not only mis-
took another person for your daughter ; but the
very servant of whom I made mention, and who
gave me so exact a description of this castle, was,
according to what you say, some other person!'

"'My dear Marino, that servant was some cheat
who knew this castle, and who, God only knows
for what motive, spoke to you of my daughter as
resembling the lady.'

"''Tis certainly no wish of mine to contradict
you ; but Ida's features are precisely the same as
those which made so deep an impression on me at
Paris, and which my imagination has preserved
with such scrupulous fidelity.'

"The count shook his head; and Marino continued :—

"'What is still more—(but pray pardon me for
mentioning a little particularity, which nothing
short of necessity would have drawn from me)—
while in the gallery, I was standing behind the lady, and the handkerchief that covered her neck was
a little disarranged, which occasioned me distinctly
to perceive the mark of a small strawberry.'

"' Another strange mystery!' exclaimed the
count, turning pale : ' it appears you are determined to make me believe wonderful stories.'

"'I have only one question to ask :—Has Ida
such a mark on her neck ?'

"' No, monsieur,' replied the count, looking
steadfastly at Marino.

"' No!' exclaimed the latter, in the utmost
astonishment.

"' No, I tell you : but Ida's twin-sister, who resembled her in the most surprising manner, had the
mark you mention on her neck, and a year since
carried it with her into the grave.'

"' And yet 'tis only within the last few months
that I saw this person in Paris !'

"At this moment the countess and Ida, who had
kept aside, a prey to uneasiness, not knowing what
to think of the conversation, which appeared of so
very important a nature, approached; but the
count in a commanding tone ordered them to
retire immediately. He then led the duke entirely

away into a retired corner of the window, and continued the conversation in so low a voice that I
could hear nothing further.

"My astonishment was extreme when, that very
same evening, the count gave orders to have Hildegarde's tomb opened in his presence: but he beforehand related briefly what I have just told you,
and proposed my assisting the duke and him in
opening the grave. The duke excused himself, by
saying that the very idea made him tremble with
horror; for he could not overcome, especially at
night, his fear of a corpse.

"The count begged he would not mention the
gallery scene to any one; and above all, to spare
the extreme sensibility of the affianced bride from
a recital of the conversation they had just had,
even if she should request to be informed of it.

"In the mean time, the sexton arrived with his
lantern. The count and I followed him.

"'It is morally impossible,' said the count to
me, as we walked together, 'that any trick can have
been played respecting my daughter's death : the
circumstances attendant thereon are but too well
known to me. You may readily believe also, that
the affection we bore our poor girl would prevent
our running any risk of burying her too soon : but
suppose even the possibility of that, and that the
tomb had been opened by some avaricious persons,

who found, on opening the coffin, that the body be-
came re-animated; no one can believe for a moment that my daughter would not have instantly
returned to her parents, who doted on her, rather
than have fled to a distant country. This last circumstance puts the matter beyond doubt: for even
should it be admitted as a truth, that she was carried by force to some distant part of the world,
she would have found a thousand ways of returning. My eyes are, however, about to be convinced,
that the sacred remains of my Hildegarde really
repose in the grave.

"' To convince myself!' cried he again, in a tone
of voice so melancholy yet loud that the sexton
turned his head.

"This movement rendered the count more circumspect; and he continued, in a lower tone of
voice:

"'How should I for a moment believe it possible that the slightest trace of my daughter's features
should be still in existence, or that the destruc-
tive hand of time should have spared her beauty?
Let us return, marquis; for who could tell, even
were I to see the skeleton, that I should know
it from that of an entire stranger, whom they may
have placed in the tomb to fill her place?'

"He was even about to give orders not to open
the door of the chapel, (at which we were just ar-

rived,) when I represented to him, that were I in
his place I should have found it extremely difficult to determine on such a measure; but that
having gone thus far, it was requisite to complete
the task, by examining whether some of the jewels
buried with Hildegarde's corpse were not wanting. I added, that judging by a number of well-
known facts, all bodies were not destroyed equally
soon.

" My representations had the desired effect : the
count squeezed my hand; and we followed the sexton, who, by his pallid countenance and trembling
limbs, evidently shewed that he was unaccustomed
to nocturnal employments of this nature.

" I know not whether any of this present company were ever in a chapel at midnight, before the
iron doors of a vault, about to examine the succession of leaden coffins enclosing the remains of an
illustrious family. Certain it is, that at such a moment the noise of bolts and bars produces such a
remarkable sensation, that one is led to dread the
sound of the door grating on its hinges; and when
the vault is opened, one cannot help hesitating for
an instant to enter it.

" The count was evidently seized with these sen-
sations of terror, which I discovered by a stifled
sigh; but he concealed his feelings : notwithstanding, I remarked that he dared not trust himself to

look on any other coffin than the one containing
his daughter's remains. He opened it himself.

" ';Did I not say so ?'. cried he, seeing that the ·
features of the corpse bore a perfect resemblance to
those of Ida. I was obliged to prevent the count,
who was seized with astonishment, from kissing the
forehead of the inanimate body. ·,

" ' Do not,' I added, ' disturb the peace of those
who repose in death.' And I used my utmost efforts to withdraw the count immediately from this
dismal abode.

" On our return to the castle, we found those persons whom we had left there, in an anxious state of
suspense. The two ladies had closely questioned
the duke on what had passed; and would not admit as a valid excuse, the promise he had made of
secrecy. They entreated us also, but in vain, to satisfy their curiosity.

" They succeeded better the following day with
the sexton, whom they sent for privately, and who
told them all he knew : but it only tended to excite their anxious wish to learn the subject of the
conversation which had occasioned this nocturnal
visit to the sepulchral vault.

" As for myself, I dreamt the whole of the following night of the apparition Marino had seen at
Paris; I conjectured many things which I did not
think fit to communicate to the count; because he

absolutely questioned the connection of a superior
world with ours. At this juncture of affairs, I
with pleasure saw that this singular circumstance,
if not entirely forgotten, was at least but rarely and
slightly mentioned. , ' ` , ' ` ,

" But I now began to find another cause for
anxious solicitude. The duke constantly persisted
in refusing to explain himself on the subject of his
previous engagement, even when we were alone :
and the embarrassment he could not conceal,
whenever I made mention of the good qualities
that I believed his intended to have possessed, as
well as several other little singularities, led me to
conclude that Marino's attachment for Apollonia
had been first shaken at the picture gallery, at
sight of the lovely incognita; and that Apollonia
had been forsaken, owing to his yielding to temp-
tations; and that doubtless she could never have
been guilty of breaking off an alliance so solemnly
contracted.

Foreseeing from this that the charming Ida
could never hope to find much happiness in an
union with Marino, and knowing that the wedding-
day was nigh at hand, I resolved to unmask the
perfidious deceiver as quickly as possible, and to
make him repent his infidelity. An excellent occasion presented itself one day for me, to accom-
plish my designs. Having finished supper, we

were still sitting at table; and some one said that
iniquity is frequently punished in this world: upon
which, I observed, that I myself had witnessed
striking proofs of the truth of this remark;—when
Ida and her mother entreated me to name one of
these examples.

: "'Under these circumstances, ladies,' answered
I, 'permit me to relate a history to you, which,
according to my opinion, will particularly interest
you.'

"'Us!' they both exclaimed. At the same time
I fixed my eyes on the duke, who for several days
past had evidently distrusted me; and I saw that
his conscience had rendered him pale.

"'That at least is *my* opinion,'replied I : 'But,
my dear count, will you pardon me, if the supernatural is sometimes interwoven with my narration?'

"'Very willingly,' answered he smiling : ' and
I will content myself with expressing my surprise
at so many things of this sort having happened to
you, as I have never experienced any of them myself.'

" I plainly perceived that the duke made signs of
approval at what he said: but I took no notice of
it, and answered the count by saying, .

" That all the world have not probably the use
of their eyes.

"' That may be,' replied he, still smiling.

"' But,' said I to him in a low and expressive voice, ' think you an uncorrupted body in the vault is a *common* phænomenon?'

" He appeared staggered : and I thus continued in an under tone of voice :—

"' For that matter, 'tis very possible to account for it naturally, and therefore it would be useless to contest the subject with you.'

"' We are wandering from the point,' said the countess a little.angrily; and she made me a sign to begin, which I accordingly did, in the following words :—

"' The scene of my anecdote lies in Venice.'

"' I possibly then may know something of it,' cried the duke, who entertained some suspicions.

"' Possibly so,' replied I ; ' but there were reasons for keeping the event secret : it happened somewhere about eighteen months since, at the period you first set out on your travels.

" The son of an extremely wealthy nobleman, whom I shall designate by the name of Filippo, being attracted to Leghorn by the affairs consequent on his succession to an inheritance, had won the heart of an amiable and lovely girl, called Clara. He promised her, as well as her parents, that ere his return to Venice he would come back and marry her. The moment for his departure

was preceded by certain ceremonies, which in
their termination were terrible : for after the two
lovers had exhausted every protestation of recipro-
cal affection, Filippo invoked the aid of the spirit
of vengeance, in case of infidelity : they prayed even
that whichever of the lovers should prove faithful
might not be permitted to repose quietly in the
grave, but should haunt the perjured one, and force
the inconstant party to come amongst the dead,
and to share in the grave those sentiments which
on earth had been forgotten.

" The parents, who were seated by them at table, remembered their youthful days, and permitted the overheated and romantic imagination of the
young people to take its free course. The lovers
finished by making punctures in their arms, and
letting their blood run into a glass filled with
white champaigne.

'.'' Our souls shall be inseparable as our blood !'
exclaimed Filippo ; and drinking half the contents
of the glass, he gave the rest to Clara."

At this moment the duke experienced a violent
degree of agitation, and from time to time
darted such menacing looks at me, that I was led
to conclude, that in *his* adventure some scene of a
similar nature had taken place. I can however
affirm, that I related the details respecting Filip-

po's departure, as they were represented in a letter written by the mother of Clara.

" Who," continued I, " after so many demon-
strations of such a violent passion, could have expected the denouement ? Filippo's return to Venice happened precisely at the period at which a
young beauty, hitherto educated in a distant convent, made her first appearance in the great world:
she on a sudden exhibited herself as an angel whom
a cloud had till then concealed, and excited universal admiration. Filippo's parents had heard frequent mention of Clara, and of the projected alliance between her and their son; but they thought
that this alliance was like many others, contracted
one day without the parties knowing why, and
broken off the next with equal want of thought;
and influenced by this idea, they presented their
son to the parents of Camilla, (which was the name
of the young beauty,) whose family were of the
highest rank.

" They represented to Filippo the great advantages he would obtain by an alliance with her.
The Carnival happening just at this period completed the business, by affording him so many favourable opportunities of being with Camilla; and
in the end, the remembrance of Leghorn held but
very little place in his mind. His letters became

colder and colder each succeeding day; and on Clara expressing how sensibly she felt the change, he ceased writing to her altogether, and did every thing in his power to hasten his union with Camilla, who was, without compare, much the handsomer and more wealthy. The agonies poor Clara endured were manifest in her illegible writing, and by the tears which were but too evidently shed over her letters: but neither the one nor the other had any more influence over the fickle heart of Filippo, than the prayers of the unfortunate girl. Even the menace of coming, according to their solemn agreement, from the tomb to haunt him, and carry him with her to that grave which threatened so soon to enclose her, had but little effect on his mind, which was entirely engrossed by the idea of the happiness he should enjoy in the arms of Camilla.

"The father of the latter (who was my intimate friend) invited me before-hand to the wedding; And although numerous affairs detained him that summer in the city, so that he could not as usual enjoy the pleasures of the country, yet we sometimes went to his pretty villa, situated on the banks of the Brenta; where his daughter's marriage was to be celebrated with all possible splendour.

"A particular circumstance, however, occasioned the ceremony to be deferred for some weeks.

The parents of Camilla having been very happy in
their own union, were anxious that the same priest
who married them, should pronounce the nuptial
benediction on their daughter. This priest, who,
notwithstanding his great age, had the appearance
of vigorous health, was seized with a slow fever
which confined him to his bed : however, in time it
abated, he became gradually better and better,
and the wedding-day was at length fixed. But,
as if some secret power was at work to prevent
this union, the worthy priest was, on the very day
destined for the celebration of their marriage,
seized with a feverish shivering of so alarming a
nature, that he dared not stir out of the house, and
he strongly advised the young couple to select another priest to marry them.

" The parents still persisted in their design of
the nuptial benediction being given to their children by the respectable old man who had married
them.—They would have certainly spared themselves a great deal of grief, if they had never
swerved from their determination.—Very grand
preparations had been made in honour of the day;
and as they could no longer be deferred, it was decided that they should consider it as a ceremony
of solemn affiance. At noon the bargemen attired
in their splendid garb awaited the company's arrival on the banks of the canal : their joyous song

'was soon distinguished, while conducting to the
villa, now decorated with flowers, the numerous
gondolas containing parties of the best company.
; "During the dinner, which lasted till evening,
the betrothed couple exchanged rings. At the
very moment of their so doing, a piercing shriek was
heard, which struck terror into the breasts of all
the company, and absolutely struck Filippo with
horror. Every one ran to the windows : for although it was becoming dark, each object was visible; but no one was to be seen."

"Stop an instant," said the duke to me, with a
fierce smile—His countenance, which had frequently
changed colour during the recital, evinced strong
marks of the torments of a wicked conscience.
" I am also acquainted with that story, of a voice
being heard in the air; it is borrowed from the
' Memoirs of Mademoiselle Clairon;' a deceased
lover tormented her in this completely original
manner. The shriek in her case was followed by a
clapping of hands: I hope, monsieur le marquis,
that you will not omit that particular in your story."

" And why," replied I, " should you imagine
that nothing of a similar nature could occur to any
one besides that actress? Your incredulity appears
to me so much the more extraordinary, as it seems
to rest on facts which may lay claim to belief."

,The countess made me a sign to continue; and I pursued my narrative as follows:

" A short time after they had heard this inexplicable shriek, I begged Camilla, facing whom I was sitting, to permit me to look at her ring once more, the exquisite workmanship of which had already been much admired. But it was not on her finger : a general search was made, but not the slightest trace of the ring could be discovered. The company even rose from their seats to look for it, but all in vain.

" Meanwhile, the time for the evening's amusements approached : fire-works were exhibited on the Brenta preceding the ball; the company were masked and got into the gondolas; but nothing was so striking as the silence which reigned during this *fête*; no one seemed inclined to open their mouth; and scarcely was heard a faint exclamation of *Bravo*, at sight of the fire-works.

" The ball was one of the most brilliant I ever witnessed : the precious stones and jewels with which the ladies of the party were covered, reflected the lights in the chandeliers with redoubled lustre. The most splendidly attired of the whole was Camilla. Her father, who was fond of pomp, rejoiced in the idea that no one in the assembly was equal to his daughter in splendour or beauty.

" Possibly to satisfy himself of this fact, he made a tour of the room; and returned loudly expressing his surprise, at having perceived on another lady precisely the same jewels which adorned Camilla. He was even weak enough to express a slight degree of chagrin. However, he consoled himself with the idea, that a bouquet of diamonds which was destined for Camilla to wear at supper, would alone in value be greater than all she then had on.

" But as they were on the point of sitting down to table, and the anxious father again threw a look around him, he discovered that the same lady had also a bouquet which appeared to the full as valuable as Camilla's.

" My friend's curiosity could no longer be restrained; he approached, and asked whether it would be too great a liberty to learn the name of the fair mask? But to his great surprise, the lady shook her head, and turned away from him.

" At the same instant the steward came in, to ask whether since dinner there had been any addition to the party, as the covers were not sufficient.

" His master answered, with rather a dissatisfied air, that there were only the same number, and accused his servants of negligence; but the steward still persisted in what he had said.

" An additional cover was placed: the master counted them himself, and discovered that there really was one more in number than he had invited. As he had recently, on account of some inconsiderate expressions, had a dispute with government, he was apprehensive that some spy had contrived to slip in with the company: but as he had no reason to believe, that on such a day as that, any thing of a suspicious nature would be uttered, he resolved, in order to be satisfied respecting so indiscreet a procedure as the introduction of such a person in a family *fête*, to beg every one present to unmask; but in order to avoid the inconvenience likely to arise from such a request, he determined not to propose it till the very last thing.

- " Every one present expressed their surprise at the luxuries and delicacies of the table, for it far surpassed every thing of the sort seen in that country, especially with respect to the wines. Still, however, the father of Camilla was not satisfied, and loudly lamented that an accident had happened to his capital red champaigne, which prevented his being able to offer his guests a single glass of it.

" The company seemed anxious to become gay, for the whole of the day nothing like gaiety had been visible among them; but no one around where I sat, partook of this inclination, for curiosity alone appeared to occupy their whole attention. I was sitting near the lady who was so splendidly attired; and I remarked that she neither ate nor drank any thing; that she neither addressed nor answered a word to her neighbours, and that she appeared to have her eyes constantly fixed on the affianced couple.

"The rumour of this singularity gradually spread round the room, and again disturbed the mirth which had become pretty general. Each whispered to the other a thousand conjectures on this mysterious personage. But the general opinion was, that some unhappy passion, for Filippo was the cause of this extaordinary conduct. Those sitting next the unknown, were the first to rise from table, in order to find more cheerful associates, and their places were filled by others who hoped to discover some acquaintance in this silent lady, and obtain from her a more welcome reception; but their hopes were equally futile.

"At the time the champaigne was handed round, Filippo also brought a chair and sat by the unknown. She then became somewhat more animated, and turned towards Filippo, which was more than she had done to any one else; and she offered him her glass, as if wishing him to drink out of it.

" A violent trembling seized Filippo, when she looked at him steadfastly.

" ' The wine is red!' cried he, holding up the glass; 'I thought there had been no *red* champaigne.'.

" ' Red! said the father of Camilla, with an air of extreme surprise, approaching him from curiosity.

" ' Look at the lady's glass,' replied Filippo.

" ' The wine in it is as white as all the rest,' answered Camilla's father; and he called all present to witness it. They every one unanimously declared that the wine was white.

" Filippo drank it not, but quitted his seat; for a second look from his neighbour had caused him extreme agitation. He took the father of Camilla aside, and whispered something to him. The latter returned to the company, saying,

" ' Ladies and gentlemen, I entreat you, for reasons which I will tell you presently, instantly to unmask.'

" As in this request he but expressed in a degree the general wish, every one's mask was off as quick as thought, and each face uncovered, excepting that of the silent lady, on whom every look was fixed, and whose face they were the most anxious to see.

"'You alone keep on your mask,' said Camilla's father to her, after a short silence: 'May I hope you will also remove yours?'

" She obstinately persisted in her determination of remaining unknown.

" This strange conduct affected the father of Camilla the more sensibly, as he recognised in the others all those whom he had invited to the *fête*, and found beyond doubt that the mute lady was the one exceeding the number invited. He was, however, unwilling to force her to unmask; because the uncommon splendour of her dress did not permit him any longer to harbour the idea that this additional guest was a spy; and thinking her also a person of distinction, he did not wish to be deficient in good manners. He thought possibly she might be some friend of the family, who, not residing at Venice, but finding on her arrival in that city that he was to give this *fête*, had conceived this innocent frolic.

" It was thought right, however, at all events to obtain all the information that could be gained from the servants: but none of them knew any thing of this lady; there were no servants of hers there; and those belonging to Camilla's father did not recollect having seen any who appeared to appertain to her.

" What rendered this circumstance doubly

strange was, that, as I before mentioned, this lady
only put the magnificent bouquet into her bosom
the instant previous to her sitting down to supper.

" The whispering, which had generally usurped
the place of all conversation, gained each moment
more and more ascendancy; when on a sudden the
masked lady arose, and walking towards the door,
beckoned Filippo to follow her ; but Camilla hindered him from obeying her signal, for she had a
long time observed with what fixed attention the
mysterious lady looked at her intended husband; and
she had also remarked, that the latter had quitted
the stranger in violent agitation ; and from all
this she apprehended that love had caused him to
be guilty of some folly or other. The master of
the house, turning a deaf ear to all his daughter's
remonstrances, and a prey to the most terrible
fears, followed the unknown (at a distance, it is
true) ; but she was no sooner out of the room than
he returned. At this moment, the shriek which
they had heard at noon was repeated, but seemed
louder from the silence of night, and communicated anew affright to all present. By the
time the father of Camilla had returned from
the first movement which his fear had occasioned
him to make, the unknown was no where to be
found.

" The servants in waiting outside the house had

no knowledge whatever of the masked lady. In every direction around there were crowds of per- sons; the river was lined with gondolas ; and yet not an individual among them had seen the myste- rious female.

" All these circumstances had occasioned so much uneasiness to the whole party, that every one was anxious to return home; and the master of the house was obliged to permit the departure of the gondolas much earlier than he had intended.

" The return home was, as might naturally be expected, very melancholy.

" On the following day the betrothed couple were, however, pretty composed. Filippo had even adopted Camilla's idea of the unknown being some one whom love had deprived of reason; and as for the horrible shriek twice repeated, they were willing to attribute it to some people who were di- verting themselves; and they decided, that inatten- tion on the part of the servants was the sole cause of the unknown absenting herself without being perceived; and they even at last persuaded them- selves, that the sudden disappearance of the ring, which they had not been able to find, was owing to the malice of some one of the servants who had pilfered it.

" In a word, they banished every thing that could tend to weaken these explanations; and only

one thing remained to harass them. The old
priest, who was to bestow on them the nuptial benediction, had yielded up his last breath ; and the
friendship which had so intimately subsisted between him and the parents of Camilla, did not permit them in decency to think of marriage and
amusements the week following his death.

"The day this venerable priest was buried, Filippo's gaiety received a severe shock ; for he
learned, in a letter from Clara's mother, the death
of that lovely girl. Sinking under the grief occasioned her by the infidelity of the man she had
never ceased to love, she died : but to her latest
hour she declared she should never rest quietly in
her grave, until the perjured man had fulfilled the
promise he had made to her.

" This circumstance produced a stronger effect
on him than all the imprecations of the unhappy
mother ; for he recollected that the first shriek
(the cause of which they had never been able to
ascertain) was heard at the precise moment of Clara's death ; which convinced him that the unknown
mask could only have been the spirit of Clara.

" This idea deprived him at intervals of his
senses.

" He constantly carried this letter about him ;
and with an air of wandering would sometimes
draw it from his pocket, in order to reconsider it

attentively : even Camilla's presence did not deter
him.

" As it was natural to conclude this letter contained the cause of the extraordinary change which
had taken place in Filippo, she, one day gladly
seized the opportunity of reading it, when in one
of his absent fits he let it fall from his hands.

" Filippo, struck by the death-like paleness and
faintness which overcame Camilla, as she returned
him the letter, knew instantly that she had read it.
In the deepest affliction he threw himself at her
feet, and conjured her to tell him how he must
act.

" ' Love me with greater constancy than you did
her,'—replied Camilla mournfully.

" With transport he promised to do so. But
his agitation became greater and greater, and increased to a most extraordinary pitch the morning
of the day fixed for the wedding. As he was going to the house of Camilla's father before it became dark, (from whence he was to take his bride
at dawn of day to the church, according to the
custom of the country,) he fancied he saw Clara's
spirit walking constantly at his side.

" Never was seen a couple about to receive
the nuptial benediction, with so mournful an aspect.
I accompanied the parents of Camilla, who had
requested me to be a witness : and the sequel has

made an indelible impression on my mind of the
events of that dismal morning.

" We were proceeding silently to the church of
the Salutation; when Filippo, in our way thither,
frequently requested me to remove the stranger
from Camilla's side, for she had evil designs
against her.

" ' What stranger ?' I asked him.

" ' In God's name, don't speak so loud,' replied
he; ' for you cannot but see how anxious she is to
force herself between Camilla and me.'

" ' Mere chimera, my friend; there are none but
yourself and Camilla.'

" ' Would to Heaven my eyes did not deceive
me !'—' Take care that she does not enter the
church,' added he, as we arrived at the door.

" ' She will not enter it, rest assured,' said I:
and to the great astonishment of Camilla's parents I made a motion as if to drive some one
away.

" We found Filippo's father already in the
church ; and as soon as his son perceived him, he
took leave of him as if he was going to die.   Camilla sobbed; and Filippo exclaimed :—

" ' There's the stranger; she has then got in.'

" The parents of Camilla doubted whether under such circumstances the marriage ceremony
ought to be begun.

" But Camilla, entirely devoted to her love, cried :—' These chimeras of fancy render my care and attention the more necessary.'

"'They approached the altar. At that moment a sudden gust of wind blew out the wax-tapers. The priest appeared displeased at their not having shut the windows more securely; but Filippo exclaimed: ' The windows! See you not, then, that there is one here who blew out the wax-tapers purposely ?'

" Every one looked astonished : and Filippo cried, as he hastily disengaged his hand from that of Camilla,—' Don't you see, also, that she is tearing me away from my intended bride ?'

" Camilla fell fainting into the arms of her parents; and the priest declared, that under such peculiar circumstances it was impossible to proceed with the ceremony.

" The parents of both attributed Filippo's state to mental derangement. They even supposed he had been poisoned; for an instant after, the unfortunate man expired in most violent convulsions. The surgeons who opened his body could not, however, discover any grounds for this suspicion.

" The parents, who as well as myself were informed by Camilla of the subject of these sup-

M

posed horrors of Filippo, did every thing in their
power to conceal this adventure : yet, on talking
over all the circumstances, they could never satis-
factorily explain the apparition of the mysterious
mask at the time of the wedding *fête*. And what
still appeared very surprising was, that the ring lost
at the country villa was found amongst Camilla's
other jewels, at the time of their return from
church."

"'This is, indeed, a wonderful history!' said
the count. His wife uttered a deep sigh : and Ida
exclaimed,—

"'It has really made *me* shudder.'

"'That is precisely what every betrothed person
ought to feel who listens to such recitals,' answered I, looking steadfastly at the duke, who,
while I was talking, had risen and sat down again
several times; and who, from his troubled look,
plainly shewed that he feared I should counteract
his wishes.

"'A word with you!' he whispered me, as we
were retiring to rest : and he accompanied me to
my room. 'I plainly perceive your generous intentions; this history invented for the occasion—"

"'Hold!' said I to him in an irritated tone of
voice : 'I was eye-witness to what you have just
heard. How then can you doubt its authenticity,

without accusing a man of honour of uttering a
falsehood ?'

, " ' We will talk on this subject presently;' replied he in a tone of raillery. ' But tell me truly
from whence you learnt the anecdote, relative to
mixing the blood with wine ?—I know the person
from whose life you borrowed this idea.'

" ' I do assure you that I have taken it from no
one's life but Filippo's; and yet there may be similar stories—as of the shriek, for instance. But even
this singular manner of irrevocably affiancing themselves may have presented itself to *any* two lovers.'

" ' Perhaps so ! Yet one could trace in your narration many traits resembling another history.'

" ' That is very possible : all love-stories are
founded on the same stock, and cannot deny their
parentage.'

" ' No matter,' replied Marino ; ' but I desire
that from henceforth you do not permit yourself
to make any allusion to my past life ; and still less
that you relate certain anecdotes to the count. On
these conditions, and only on these conditions, do
I pardon your former very ingenious fiction.'

" ' Conditions !——forgiveness !——And do you
dare thus to talk to *me* ?——This is rather too
much. Now take my answer : To-morrow morning the count shall know that you have been already affianced, and what you now exact.'

M 2

"' Marquis, if you dare——'

"Oh! oh!—yes, I dare do it; and I owe it to an old friend. The impostor who dares accuse me of falsehood shall no longer wear his deceitful mask in this house.'

" Passion had, spite of my endeavours, carried me so far, that a duel became inevitable. The duke challenged me. And we agreed, at parting, to meet the following morning in a neighbouring wood with pistols.

" In effect, before day-light we each took our servant and went into the forest. Marino, remarking that I had not given any orders in case of my being killed, undertook to do so for me; and accordingly he told my servant what to do with my body, as if every thing was already decided. He again addressed me ere we shook hands;—

"' For,' said he, ' the combat between us must be very unequal. I am young,' added he ; ' but in many instances my hand has proved a steady one. I have not, it is true, absolutely killed any man; but I have invariably hit my adversary precisely on the part I intended. In this instance, however, I must, for the first time, *kill* my man, as it is the only effectual method of preventing your annoying me further; unless you will give me your word of honour not to discover any occurrences of my past life to

the count, in which case I consent to consider the
affair as terminated here.'

"As you may naturally believe, I rejected his
proposition.

"' As it must be so,' replied he, ' recommend
your soul to God.' We prepared accordingly.

"' It is your first fire,' he said to me.

"' I yield it to you,' answered I.

"He refused to fire first. I then drew the trigger,
and caused the pistol to drop from his hand. He
appeared surprised : but his astonishment was
great indeed, when, after taking up another pistol,
he found he had missed me. He pretended to
have aimed at my heart; and had not even the possibility of an excuse; for he could not but acknow-
ledge that no sensation of fear on my part had
induced me to move, and baulk his aim.

"At his request I fired a second time ; and again
aimed at his pistol which he held in his left hand:
and to his great astonishment it dropped also ; but
the ball had passed so near his hand, that it was a
good deal bruised.

"His second fire having passed me, I told him
I would not fire again ; but that, as it was possible
the extreme agitation of his mind had occasioned him to miss me twice, I proposed adjusting
matters.

"Before he had time to refuse my offer, the

count, who had suspicions that all was not right,
was between us, with his daughter. He complained
loudly of such conduct on the part of his guests;
and demanded some explanation on the cause of
our dispute. I then developed the whole business in presence of Marino, whose evident embarrassment convinced the count and Ida of the truth
of the reproaches his conscience made him.

"But the duke soon availed himself of Ida's affection, and created an entire change in the count's
mind; who that very evening said to me,—

"'You are right; I certainly ought to take some
decided step, and send the duke from my house:
but what could win the Apollonia whom he has
abandoned; and whom he will never see again?
Added to which, he is the only man for whom my
daughter has ever felt a sincere attachment. Let
us leave the young people to follow their own inclinations: the countess perfectly coincides in this
opinion; and adds, that it would hurt her much
were this handsome Venetian to be driven from our
house. How many little infidelities and indiscre-
tions are committed in the world and excused,
owing to particular circumstances?'

"'But it appears to me, that in the case in point,
these particular circumstances are wanting,' answered I. However, finding the count persisted
in his opinion, I said no more.

' :" The marriage took place without any interruption: but still there was very little of gaiety at the
feast, which usually on these occasions is of so
splendid and jocund a nature. · The ball in the
evening was dull; and Marino alone danced with
most extraordinary glee.

· " ' Fortunately, monsieur le marquis,' said he
in my ear, quitting the dance for an instant and
laughing aloud, " there are no ghosts or spirits
here, as at your Venetian wedding.' : ‹

: " ' Don't,' I answered, putting up my finger to
him, ' rejoice too soon: misery is slow in its ope-
rations; and often is not perceived by us blind
mortals till it treads on our heels.' · ·

· " Contrary to my intention, this conversation
rendered him quite silent ; and what convinced me
the more strongly of the effect it had made on him,
was, the redoubled vehemence with which the duke
again began dancing. . ‹

" The countess in vain entreated him to be care- .
ful of his health : and all Ida's supplications were
able to obtain was, a few minutes' rest to take
breath when he could no longer go on. ·

. "A few minutes after, I saw Ida in tears, which
did not appear as if occasioned by joy; and she
quitted the ball-room. I was standing as close to
the door as I am to you at this moment ; so that I
could not for an instant doubt its being really Ida:

but what appeared to me very strange was, that in
a few seconds I saw her come in again with a countenance as calm as possible. I followed her, and
remarked that she asked the duke to dance; and
was so far from moderating his violence, that she
partook of and even increased it by her own example. I also remarked, that as soon as the dance
was over the duke took leave of the parents of
Ida, and with her vanished through a small door
leading to the nuptial apartment.

" While I was endeavouring to account in my
own mind how it was possible for Ida so suddenly
to change her sentiments, a conference in an under-
tone took place at the door of the room, between
the count and his valet.

" The subject was evidently a very important
one, as the greatly incensed looks of the count towards his gardener evinced, while he confirmed, as
it appeared, what the valet had before said.

" I drew near the trio, and heard, that at a particular time the church organ was heard to play,
and that the whole edifice had been illuminated
within, until twelve o'clock, which had just struck.

" The count was very angry at their troubling
him with so silly a tale, and asked why they did not
sooner inform him of it. They answered, that every
one was anxious to see how it would end. The
gardener added, that the old chaplain had been

seen again; and the peasantry who lived near the
forest, even pretended that they had seen the sum-
mit of the mountain which overhung their valley
illuminated, and spirits dance around it. .·

" '.Very well!' exclaimed the count with· a
gloomy air ; 'so all the old idle trash is resumed :
the *Death-Bride* is also, I hope, going to play her
part.'

" The valet having pushed aside the gardener,
that he might not still further enrage the count, I
put in my word; and said to the count, ' You
might at least listen to what they have to say, and
learn what it is they pretend to have seen.'

. " ' What is said about the *Death-Bride* ?' said
I to the gardener.

". He shrugged up his shoulders.

.. "' Was I not right?' cried the count : ' here we
are then, and must listen to this ridiculous tale.
All these things are treasured in the memory of
these people, and constantly afford· subjects and
phantoms to their imaginations.——Is it permitted
to ask under what form ?'——

" ' Pray pardon me,' replied the gardener ; ' but
it resembled the deceased mademoiselle Hildegarde. She passed close to me in the garden, and
then came into the castle.".

" ' O !' said the count to him, ' I beg, in future you will be a little more circumspect in your

fancies, and leave my daughter to rest quietly in
the tomb——'Tis well—'

"He then made a signal to his servants, who
went out.

"'Well! my dear marquis!' said he to me.

"'Well?'

"'Your belief in stories will not, surely, carry
you so far as to give credence to my Hildegarde's
spirit appearing?'

"'At least it may have appeared to the gardener
only——Do you recollect the adventure in the
Museum at Paris?'

"'You are right: that again was a pretty invention, which to this moment I cannot fathom. Believe me, I should sooner have refused my daughter to the duke for his having been the fabricator
of so gross a story, than for his having forsaken his
first love.'

"'I see very plainly that we shall not easily accord on this point; for if my ready belief appears
strange to you, your doubts seem to me incomprehensible.'

"The company assembled at the castle, retired
by degrees; and I alone was left with the count
and his lady, when Ida came to the room-door,
clothed in her ball-dress, and appeared astonished
at finding the company had left.

"'What can this mean?' demanded the countess. Her husband could not find words to express his astonishment.

" ' Where is Marino ?' exclaimed Ida.

" ' Do *you* ask us where he is ?' replied her mother; ' did we not see you go out with him through that small door ?'

" ' That could not be ;—you mistake.'

" ' No, no; my dear child! A very short time since you were dancing with singular vehemence; and then you both went out together.'

" ' *Me!* my mother ?'

" ' Yes, my dear Ida: how is it possible you should have forgotten all this ?'

" ' I have forgotten nothing, believe me.'

" ' Where then have you been all this time ?'

" ' In my sister's chamber,' said Ida.

" I remarked that at these words the count became somewhat pale; and his fearful eye caught mine : he however said nothing. The countess, fearing that her daughter was deceiving her, said to her in an afflicted tone of voice :—

" ' How could so singular a fancy possess you on a day like this ?'

" ' I cannot account for it; and only know, that all on a sudden I felt an oppression at my heart, and fancied that all I wanted was Hildegarde. At the same time I felt a firm belief that I should find her in her room playing on her guitar; for which reason I crept thither softly.'

"'And did you find her there?'

"'Alas! no: but the eager desire that I felt to see her, added to the fatigue of dancing, so entirely overpowered me, that I seated myself on a chair, where I fell fast asleep.'

"'How long since did you quit the room?'

"'The clock in the tower struck the three-quarters past eleven just as I entered my sister's room.'

"'What does all this mean?' said the countess to her husband in a low voice: 'she talks in a connected manner; and yet I know, that as the clock struck three-quarters past eleven, I entreated Ida on this very spot to dance more moderately.'

"'And Marino?'—asked the count.

"'I thought, as I before said, that I should find him here.'

"'Good God!' exclaimed the mother, 'she raves: but the duke—Where is he then?'

"'What then, my good mother?' said Ida with an air of great disquiet, while leaning on the countess.

"Meanwhile the count took a wax-taper, and made a sign for me to follow him. A horrible spectacle awaited us in the bridal-chamber, whither he conducted me. We there found the duke extended on the floor. There did not appear the slightest signs of life in him ; and his features were distorted in the most frightful manner.

"Imagine the extreme affliction Ida endured when she heard this recital, and found that all the resources of the medical attendants were employed in vain.

"The count and his family could not be roused from the deep consternation which threatened to overwhelm them. A short time after this event, some business of importance occasioned me to quit their castle; and certainly I was not sorry for the excuse to get away.

"But ere I left that county, I did not fail to collect in the village every possible information relative to the *Death-Bride*; whose history unfortunately, in passing from one mouth to another, experienced many alterations. It appeared to me, however, upon the whole, that this affianced bride lived in this district, about the fourteenth or fifteenth century. She was a young lady of noble family, and she had conducted herself with so much perfidy and ingratitude towards her lover, that he died of grief; but afterwards, when she was about to marry, he appeared to her the night of her intended wedding, and she died in consequence. And it is said, that since that time, the spirit of this un-

fortunate creature wanders on earth in every possible shape; particularly in that of lovely females,
to render their lovers inconstant.

"As it was not permitted for her to appear in
the form of any living being, she always chose
amongst the dead those who the most strongly resembled them. It was for this reason she voluntarily frequented the galleries in which were hung
family portraits. It is even reported that she has
been seen, in galleries of pictures open to public
inspection. Finally, it is said, that, as a punishment for her perfidy, she will wander till she finds
a man whom she will in vain endeavour to make
swerve from his engagement; and it appears, they
added, that as yet she had not succeeded.

" Having inquired what connection subsisted between this spirit and the old chaplain (of whom
also I had heard mention), they informed me, that
the fate of the last depended on the young lady,
because he had assisted her in her criminal conduct. But no one was able to give me any satisfactory information concerning the voice which
had called the duke by his name, nor on the meaning of the church being illuminated at night; and
why the grand mass was chanted. No one either
knows how to account for the dance on the mountain's top in the forest.

"For the rest," added the marquis, "you will own, that the traditions are admirably adapted to my story, and may, to a certain degree, serve to fill up the gaps; but I am not enabled to give a more satisfactory explanation. I reserve for another time a second history of this same *Death-Bride*; I only heard it a few weeks since: it appears to me interesting; but it is too late to begin to-day, and indeed, even now, I fear that I have intruded too long on the leisure of the company present by my narrative."

He had just finished these words, and some of his auditors (though all thanked him for the trouble he had taken) were expressing their disbelief of the story; when a person of his acquaintance came into the room in a hurried manner, and whispered something in his ear. Nothing could be more striking than the contrast presented by the bustling and uneasy air of the newly arrived person while speaking to the marquis, and the calm air of the latter while listening to him.

"Haste, I pray you," said the first (who appeared quite out of patience at the marquis's *sang-froid*): "In a few moments you will have cause to repent this delay."

"I am obliged to you for your affecting solicitude," replied the marquis; who in taking up his hat, appeared more to do, as all the rest of the party were doing, in preparing to return home, than from any anxiety of hastening away.

" You are lost," said the other, as he saw an officer enter the room at the head of a detachment of military, who inquired for the marquis. The latter instantly made himself known to him.

" You are my prisoner," said the officer. The marquis followed him, after saying Adieu with a smiling air to all the party, and begging they would not feel any anxiety concerning him.

" Not feel anxiety !" replied he whose advice he had neglected. " I must inform you, that they have discovered that the marquis has been detected in a connection with very suspicious characters; and his death-warrant may be considered as signed. I came in pity to warn him of his danger, for possibly he might then have escaped; but from his conduct since, I can scarely imagine he is in his proper senses."

The party, who were singularly affected by this event, were conjecturing a thousand things, when the officer returned, and again asked for the marquis.

" He just now left the room with you," answered some one of the company.

" But he came in again."

"We have seen no one."

"He has then disappeared," replied the officer, smiling: he searched every corner for the marquis, but in vain. The house was thoroughly examined, but without success; and the following day the officer quitted the baths with his soldiers, without his prisoner, and very much dissatisfied.

N

V.

THE STORM.

——" Of shapes that walk
At dead of night, and clank their chains, and wave
The torch of hell around the murderer's bed."

PLEASURES OF IMAGINATION.

ON the evening of the 12th of June 17—, a joyous party was assembled at Monsieur de Montbrun's *château* to celebrate the marriage of his
nephew, who had, in the morn of that day, led to
the altar the long-sought object of his fond attachment. The mansion, which was on this occasion
the scene of merriment, was situated in the province
of Gascony, at no very great distance from the
town of ——.

It was a venerable building, erected during the
war of the League, and consequently discovered in
its exterior some traces of that species of architecture which endeavoured to unite strength and
massiveness with domestic comfort. Situated in a
romantic, but thinly peopled district, the family of
Monsieur de Montbrun was compelled principally

to rely on itself for amusement and society. This
family consisted of the chevalier, an old soldier of
blunt but hospitable manners; his nephew the
bridegroom, whom (having no male children) he
had adopted as his son, and Mademoiselle Emily,
his only daughter: the latter was amiable, frank,
and generous; warm in her attachments, but rather
romantic in forming them. Employed in rural
sports and occupations, and particularly attached
to botany, for which the country around afforded
an inexhaustible field, the chevalier and his in-
mates had not much cultivated the intimacy of
the few families which disgust to the world or
other motives had planted in this retired spot.
Occasional visits exchanged with the nearest of
their neighbours sometimes enlivened their small
circle; with the greater part of those who lived at
a distance, they were scarcely acquainted even by
name.

The approaching nuptials, however, of Theodore
(which was the name of Monsieur de Montbrun's
adopted son) excited considerable conversation
in the adjacent district: and the wedding of her
cousin, it was determined by Emily, should not
pass off unaccompanied by every festivity which
the nature of their situation and the joyfulness of
the event would allow. On this occasion, therefore, inquiries were made as to all the neighbour-

ing gentry within a considerable distance around; and there were none of the least note neglected in the invitations, which were scattered in all direc- tions. Many persons were consequently present, with whose persons and character the host and his family were unacquainted : some also accepted the summons, who were strangers to them even in name.

Emily was attentive and courteous to all; but to one lady in particular she attached herself during the entertainment with most sedulous regard. Ma- dame de Nunez, the immediate object of Emily's care, had lately settled in the neighbourhood, and had hitherto studied to shun society. It was sup- posed that she was the widow of a Spanish officer of the Walloon guards, to whom she had been fondly attached ; indeed so much so, that, not- withstanding he had been dead several years, the lady never appeared but in the garb of mourning. She had only lately settled in Gascony ; but her motives for retiring from Spain and fixing on the French side of the Pyrenees were not known, and but slightly conjectured. Isabella de Nunez was about twenty-eight years of age, tall and well- formed: her countenance was striking; nay even handsome; but a nice physiognomist would have traced in her features evidence of the stronger pas- sions of human nature. He would have seen pride

softened by distress; and would have fancied, at
times, that the effects of some concealed crime were
still evident in her knit brow and retiring eye, when
she became the object of marked scrutiny. ;
  She had never before entered the *château* de
Montbrun, and her person had hitherto been un-
noticed by Emily; but who, having now seen her,
devoted herself with ardour to her new friend.
The lady received the attentions of her amiable
hostess with grateful but dignified reserve. ·

  The morning had been extremely sultry, and an
oppressive sensation in the air, which disordered
respiration, threw, as the day closed, an air of
gloom over the company, ill suited to the occasion
of their meeting. Madame de Nunez appeared
more than any one else to feel the effects of the
lurid atmosphere ; the occasional sparks of gaiety
which she had discovered, gradually disappeared ;
and before the day had entirely shut in, she seemed
at times perfectly abstracted, at other times to
start with causeless apprehension. In order to divert or dispel this increasing uneasiness, which
threatened to destroy all the pleasure of the festi-
val, dancing was proposed; and the enlivening
sounds of the music in a short time dissipated the
temporary gloom. The dancing had not however
long continued, ere the expected storm burst in all
its fury on the *château :* the thunder, with its con-

tinued roar, reverberated by the adjoining mountains, caused the utmost alarm in the bosom of the
fair visitors ; the torrents of rain which fell, might
almost be said to swell the waters of the neighbouring Garonne, whilst sheets of lightning, reflected
on its broad waves, gave a deeper horror to the
pitchy darkness which succeeded. The continuance
of the storm gradually wound up the apprehensions of the greater part of the females to horror;
and they took refuge in the arched vaults, and long
subterranean passages which branched beneath the
château, from the vivid glare of the lightning ; although unable to shut their ears to the reiterated
claps of thunder which threatened to shake the
building to its foundations. In this general scene
of horror, Isabella alone appeared unappall-
ed. The alternate abstraction and alarm, which
before seemed to harass her mind, had now
vanished, and had given place to a character of
resignation which might almost be considered as
bordering on apathy. While the younger females
yielded without resistance to the increasing horrors
of the tempest, and by frequent shrieks and exclamations of dread bore testimony to the terror
excited in their bosoms by the aggravated circumstances of the scene, she suffered no symptom of
apprehension to be visible in her now unvarying
features. Agitation had yielded to quiet: she sat

ostensibly placid; but her apparent inattention was
evidently not the effect of tranquillity, but the result of persevering exertion.

The hour was approaching towards midnight;
and the storm, instead of blowing over, having increased in violence, the hospitable owner of the
mansion proposed to his guests, that they should
abandon the idea of returning home through the
torrents of rain, which had already deluged the
country, and rendered the roads in the vicinity im-
passable; but should accommodate themselves,
with as little difficulty as possible, to the only plan
now to be devised,—of making themselves easy
during the remainder of this dismal night. Although his mansion was not extensive, yet he proposed '(with the aid of temporary couches, and
putting the ladies to the inconvenience of sleeping
two in each room) to render the party as comfortable as his means would allow; and which would,
at all events, be more agreeable than braving
abroad the horrors of the tempest.

Reasonable as such a plan was in itself, it was
still more strongly recommended by the circumstance, that the carriages which were expected to
convey the parties to their respective abodes had
not arrived; and from the state of the roads, and
the continuance of the still pitiless storm, it seemed
visionary to expect them.

The party, therefore, yielded without regret to the offered arrangement, save with one dissenting voice. The fair Spaniard alone positively declined the offered accommodation. Argument in vain was used for a considerable space of time to detain her; she positively insisted on returning home: and would alone in the dark have faced the storm, had not an obstacle which appeared invincible, militated against her resolve; this was too imperious to be resisted—her carriage and servants were not arrived; and from the representation of Monsieur de Montbrun's domestics (some of whom had been detached to examine the condition of the neighbouring roads), it was perfectly clear, that with that part of the district in which she resided, no communication could for several hours take place. Madame de Nunez, therefore, at length yielded to necessity; although the pertinacity of her resistance had already excited much surprise, and called forth innumerable conjectures.

The arrangements between the respective parties were soon made, and the greater part of the ladies gladly retired to seek repose from the harassing events of the day. Emily, who had not relaxed in her marked attention to her interesting friend, warmly pressed her to share her own room, in which a sopha had been prepared as a couch, and to which she herself insisted on retiring,

While madame de Nunez should take possession of the bed. The latter, however, again strenuously objected to this plan, asserting, that she should prefer remaining all night in one of the sitting-rooms, with no other companion than a book. She appeared obstinately to adhere to this resolution, until Emily politely, yet positively, declared, that were such the intention of her new friend, she would also join her in the saloon, and pass the time in conversation until the day should break, or until Madame's servants should arrive. This proposition, or rather determination, was received by the frowning Isabella with an air of visible chagrin and disappointment, not altogether polite. She expressed her unwillingness that Mademoiselle should be inconvenienced, with some peevishness; but which, however, soon gave place to her former air of good-breeding.

She now appeared anxious to hurry to her room; and the rest of the party having some time retired, she was escorted thither by the ever-attentive Emily. No sooner had they reached the chamber, than Isabella sunk into a chair; and after struggling for some time in evident emotion for utterance, at length exclaimed:—

" Why, dearest Emily, would you insist on sharing with me the horrors of this night? To me the punishment is a merited one: but, to you——"

" What, my dearest madam, do you say ?" replied Emily affectionately—" The terrors of the
night are over, the thunder appears retiring, and
the lightning is less vivid; and see in the west
(added she, as she went to the window) there are
still some remains of the summer twilight. Do not
any longer, then, suffer the apprehension of the
storm which has passed over us, to disturb the repose which you will, I hope, so shortly enjoy."

" Talk you of repose !" said Madame de Nunez,
in a voice almost choked with agitation—" Know
you not, then, that on the anniversary of this horrid
night ?——but what am I saying!—to you, at present, all this is mystery ; too soon your own feelings will add conviction to the terrible experience
which six revolving years have afforded me, and
which, even now but to think on, harrows up my
soul.—But no more—."

Then darting suddenly towards the door, which
had hitherto remained a-jar, she closed it with violence; and locking it, withdrew the key, which she
placed in her own pocket.—Emily had scarcely
time to express her surprise at this action and the
apparent distraction which accompanied it, ere
Madame de Nunez seized both her hands with
more than female strength, and with a maddened
voice and eye straining on vacancy, exclaimed :—

" Bear witness, ye powers of terror ! that I im-

posed not this dreadful scene on the female whose
oath must now secure her silence."

Then staring wildly on Mademoiselle de Montbrun, she continued :—

" Why, foolish girl, wouldst thou insist on my
partaking thy bed? the viper might have coiled
in thy bosom ; the midnight assassin might have
aimed his dagger at thy breast—but the poison of
the one would have been less fatal, and the apprehension of instant annihilation from the other
would have been less oppressive, than the harrow-
ing scene which thou art doomed this night to
witness—Doomed, I say; for all the powers of hell,
whose orgies you must behold, cannot release you
from the spectacle which you have voluntarily
sought."

"To *what* am I doomed!" cried Emily, whose
fears for herself were lessened in the dread she felt
for her friend's intellects, which she supposed were
suddenly become affected by illness, or from the
incidents of the past day.

Isabella, after a silence of several minutes, during which she endeavoured to recover some degree
of composure, in a softened but determined voice,
said :—

" Think not, my friend, (if I may use that endearing expression to one whose early prospects
and happier days I am unwillingly condemned to

blast,) that disorder has produced the agitation
which, spite of myself, you have witnessed.—Alas!
great as have been my sorrows, and heavy as my
crime weighs on me, my reason has still preserved
its throne: to seek oblivion in idiotcy; to bury the
remembrance of my fatal error in temporary derangement; would, I might almost say, be happiness
to me. But fate has forbidden such an alleviation,
and my impending destiny is not to be guarded
against by precaution, cannot be avoided by re-
pentance."

" Nay," said Emily, " exaggerated as your self-
condemnation makes the fault to which you allude
appear, in religion you may find a solace which
could efface crimes of much deeper dye than any
with which you can possibly charge yourself."

" Ah ! no," replied the fair Spaniard.—" Religion, it is true, holds out her benignant hand to
receive the wandering sinner ;—she offers to the
stranger a home ; she welcomes to her bosom the
repentant though blood-stained criminal ;—but
·for crimes like mine, what penitence can atone ?—
But we waste time," added she ; " the midnight
hour approaches ; and ere the clock in the turret
first announces that dreaded period, much must be
done."

Thus saying, she went into the adjoining oratory,
and finding on the little altar at which Emily of-

fered her daily oraisons, an ivory crucifix, she returned with it in her hand; and again seizing and
forcibly grasping the hand of her now really alarmed hostess, she exclaimed in a hollow, yet determined voice:—

"Swear, that whatsoever you may this night,
this eventful night, be a witness to, not all the apprehensions of hell, not all your hopes of heaven,
shall tempt you to reveal, until I am committed to
the silent tomb—Swear!"

Emily for a moment hesitated to adopt an oath
imposed under circumstances of such an extraordinary nature: but whilst she was debating, Madame
de Nunez, more violently grasping her hand, exclaimed, in a voice harsh from agitation:—

"Swear; or dread the event!"

"Swear!" Emily fancied she heard echoed
from the oratory. Almost sinking with horror,
she faintly repeated the solemn oath, which the
frantic female, whose character appeared so perfectly changed, thus dictated to her.

She had no sooner thus solemnly bound herself
to silence, than Madame de Nunez's agitation appeared to subside; she replaced the crucifix on the
altar, and sinking on her knees before the chair in
which Emily, almost void of animation, was seated,
she feebly exclaimed:—

"Pardon, dearest Emily, the madness of my

conduct; necessity has dictated it towards you; and
your wayward fate, and not your suffering friend, is
answerable for it. For six long years have I confined to my own bosom the horrors which we this
night must jointly witness. On the anniversary of
this day—But I dare not yet communicate the
dreadful event; some hours hence I *may* recover
composure to relate it: but remember your oath;
While I live, the secret is buried in your bosom. You
must have remarked my unwillingness to remain in
your dwelling; you could not have been inatten-
tive to my repugnance to share your room—too
soon you will have a dreadful explanation of the
cause. Be not angry with me—I must endeavour
to conceal the circumstances which appal my soul:
I must still preserve the respect of society, although I have for ever forfeited my own—hence
the oath I have imposed on you. But—"

Here further conversation was interrupted
by the sound of the turret clock, which began to
strike the hour of midnight. It had scarcely
finished, ere the slow rolling of a carriage was
heard in the paved court-yard; at the noise of
which, Madame de Nunez started from the posture
in which she had continued at the feet of Emily,
and rushed towards the door, which she had previously locked. Emily now heard heavy footsteps ascending the oaken stair-case; and before

she could recall her recollection, which so singular a circumstance had bewildered, the door of the
room in which they were sitting, spite of its fasten-
ing, slowly moved on its hinges; and in the next
minute—Emily sunk on the earth in a state of
stupefaction.

It is well for the human frame, that when as-
sailed by circumstances too powerful to support,
it seeks shelter in oblivion. The mind recoils from
the horrors which it cannot meet, and is driven
into insensibility.

At an early hour of the ensuing morning Madame de Nunez quitted Monsieur de Montbrun's
château, accompanied by her servants, whom the
retiring torrents had permitted to await their mistress's commands. She took a hasty farewell of the
master of the mansion, and without making any
inquiries as to the rest of the party, departed.

At the usual hour of breakfast, Emily did not
appear; and her father at length went to her room
door, and receiving no answer to his inquiries,
went in. Judge his horror, when he discovered his
daughter lying on the bed in the clothes she had
worn the preceding day, but in a state of apparent
insensibility. Immediate medical assistance was
procured, and she at length discovered symptoms
of returning life; but no sooner had she recovered
her recollection, than, looking with horror and af-

fright around her, she again relapsed into a state
of inanimation. Repeated cordials being admini-
stered, she was again restored to life; but only to
become the victim of a brain-fever, which in a few
days put a period to her existence. In a short
interval of recollection, in the early part of her
illness, she confided what we have here related to
her father; but conscientiously kept from his knowledge what she was bound by her oath to conceal.
The very remembrance of what she had witnessed
on that fatal night, hurried her into delirium, and
she fell a victim to the force of recollection.

Madame de Nunez did not long survive her;
but expired under circumstances of unexampled
horror.

VI.

THE SPECTRE-BARBER.

(A TALE OF THE SIXTEENTH CENTURY.)

" Sir Ryence of North-Gales greeteth well thee,
And bids thee thy beard anon to him send,
Or else from thy jaws he will it off rend."
　　　　　PERCY's *Reliques of Anc. Eng. Poetry.*

THERE formerly lived at Bremen a wealthy merchant named Melchior, who, it was remarked, invariably stroked his chin with complacency, whenever the subject of the sermon was the rich man
in the Gospel; who, by the bye, in comparison with
him, was only a petty retail dealer. This said Melchior possessed such great riches, that he had caused
the floor of his dining-room to be paved with
crown-pieces. This ridiculous luxury gave great
offence to Melchior's fellow-citizens and relations.
They attributed it to vanity and ostentation, but did
not guess its true motive: however, it perfectly answered the end Melchior designed by it; for, by their

o

constantly expressing their disapprobation of this
ostentatious species of vanity, they spread abroad
the report of their neighbour's immense riches, and
thereby augmented his credit in a most astonishing
manner.

Melchior died suddenly while at a corporation
dinner, and consequently had not time to make a
disposition of his property by will; so that his only
son Francis, who was just of age, came into possession of the whole. This young man was particularly favoured by fortune, both with respect to
his personal advantages and his goodness of heart;
but this immense inheritance caused his ruin. He
had no sooner got into the possession of so considerable a fortune, than he squandered it, as if it
had been a burthen to him; ran into every possible extravagance, and neglected his concerns. Two
or three years passed over without his perceiving,
that, owing to his dissipations, his funds were considerably diminished; but at length his coffers
were emptied: and one day when Francis had
drawn a draft to a very considerable amount on his
banker, who had no funds to meet it; it was returned to him protested. This disappointment
greatly vexed our prodigal, but only as it caused a
temporary check to his wishes; for he did not even
then give himself the trouble to inquire into the
reason of it. After swearing and blustering for

some time, he gave his steward a positive; but la-
conic order to *get money*.

All the brokers, bankers, money-changers, and
usurers, were put in requisition, and the empty
coffers were soon filled; for the dining-room
floor was in the eyes of the lenders a sufficient security.

This palliative had its effect for a time: but all
at once a report was spread abroad in the city that
the celebrated silver floor had been taken up;
the consequence of which was, that the lenders insisted on examining into and proving the fact, and
then became urgent for payment: but as Francis
had not the means to meet their demands, they
seized on all his goods and chattels; every thing
was sold by auction, and he had nothing left excepting a few jewels which had formed part of his
heritage, and which might for a short time keep
him from starving.

He now took up his abode in a small street in
one of the most remote quarters of the city,
where he lived on his straitened means. He,
however, accommodated himself to his situation:
but the only resource he found against the *ennui*
which overpowered him, was to play on the lute;
and when fatigued by this exercise, he used to
stand at his window and make observations on the

weather; and his intelligent mind was not long in
discovering an object which soon entirely engrossed
his thoughts.

- Opposite his window there lived a respectable
woman, who was at her spinning-wheel from
morning till night, and by her industry earned a
subsistence for herself and her daughter. Meta
was a young girl of great beauty and attraction : she
had known happier times; for her father had been
the proprietor of a vessel freighted by himself, in
which he annually made trading voyages to Ant-
werp: but he, as well as his ship and all its cargo,
was lost in a violent storm. His widow supported
this double loss with resignation and firmness, and
resolved to support herself and her daughter by her
own industry. She made over her house and furniture to the creditors of her husband, and took up
her abode in the little bye street in which Francis
lodged, where by her assiduity she acquired a subsistence without laying herself under an obligation
to any one. She brought up her daughter to spin-
ning and other work, and lived with so much
economy, that by her savings she was enabled to
set up a little trade in linen.

. Mother Bridget, (which was the appellation
given to our widow,) did not, however, calculate
on terminating her existence in this penurious si-

tuation; and the hope of better prospects sustained
her courage. The beauty and excellent qualities
of her daughter, whom she brought up with every
possible care and attention, led her to think that
some advantageous offer would one day present itself. Meta lived tranquilly and lonely with her mother, was never seen in any of the public walks, and
indeed never went out but to mass once a day.

    One day while Francis was making his mete-
orological observations at the window, he saw the
beautiful Meta, who, under her mother's watchful
eye, was returning from church. The heart of
Francis was as yet quite free; for the boisterous
pleasures of his past life did not leave him leisure for a true affection; but at this time, when all
his senses were calm, the appearance of one of
the most enchanting female forms he had ever seen,
ravished him, and he henceforth thought solely of
the adorable object which his eyes had thus discovered. He questioned his landlord respecting the two
females who lived in the opposite house, and from
him learned the particulars we have just related.
    He now regretted his want of economy, since his
present miserable state prevented him from making an offer to the charming Meta. He was, however, constantly at the window, in hopes of seeing
her, and in that consisted his greatest delight. The
mother very soon discovered the frequent appear-

ance of her new neighbour at his window, and attributed it to its right cause. In consequence, she
rigorously enjoined her daughter not to shew herself at the windows, which were now kept constantly shut.

Francis was not much versed in the arts of
finesse, but love awakened all the energies of his
soul. He soon discovered that if he appeared
much at the window, his views would be suspected,
and he resolved therefore studiously to refrain from
coming near it. He determined, however, to continue his observation of what occurred in the opposite dwelling without being perceived. He accordingly purchased a large mirror, and fixed it in
his chamber in such a position that it distinctly
presented to his view what passed in the abode of
his opposite neighbour. Francis not being seen at
the window, the old lady relaxed in her rigour, and
Meta's windows were once more opened. Love
more than ever reigned triumphant in the bosom
of Francis; but how was he to make known his attachment to its object? he could neither speak nor
write to her. Love, however, soon suggested a
mode of communication which succeeded. Our
prodigal took his lute, and drew from it tones the
best adapted to express the subject of his passion;
and by perseverance, in less than a month he made
a wonderful progress. He soon had the gratifica-

tion of seeing the fair hand of Meta open the little
casement, when he began to tune the instrument.
When she made her appearance, he testified his joy
by an air lively and gay; but if she did not shew
herself, the melancholy softness of his tones discovered the disappointment he experienced.

In the course of a short time he created a great
interest in the bosom of his fair neighbour; and
various modes which love suggested shortly convinced our prodigal that Meta shared a mutual attachment. She now endeavoured to justify him,
when her mother with acrimony spoke of his pro-
digality and past misconduct, by attributing his
ruin to the effect of bad example. But in so doing, she cautiously avoided exciting the suspicions
of the old lady; and seemed less anxious to excuse
him, than to take a part in the conversation which
was going on.

Circumstances which our limits will not allow us
to narrate rendered the situation of Francis more
and more difficult to be supported: his funds had
now nearly failed him; and an offer of marriage
from a wealthy brewer, who was called in the
neighbourhood the " King of Hops," and which
Meta, much to her mother's disappointment, refused, excited still more the apprehensions of poor
Francis, lest some more fortunate suitor might yet
be received, and blast his hopes for ever.

When he received the information that this opu-

lent lover had been rejected for his sake, with what
bitterness did he lament his past follies!

"Generous girl!" said he, "you sacrifice yourself for a miserable creature, who has nothing but
a heart fondly attached to you, and which is riven
with despair that its possessor cannot offer you the
happiness you so truly merit."

The King of Hops soon found another female,
who listened more kindly to his vows, and whom
he wedded with great splendour.

Love, however, did not leave his work incom-
plete ; for its influence created in the mind of
Francis a desire of exerting his faculties and ac-
tively employing himself, in order, if possible, to
emerge from the state of nothingness into which
he was at present plunged : and it inspired him
also with courage to prosecute his good intentions.
Among various projects which he formed, the most
rational appeared that of overlooking his father's
books, taking an account of the claimable debts,
and from that source to get all he possibly could.
The produce of this procedure would, he thought,
furnish him with the means of beginning in some
small way of business ; and his imagination led him
to extend this to the most remote corners of the
earth. In order to equip himself for the prosecu-
tion of his plans, he sold all the remainder of his
father's effects, and with the money purchased a
horse to commence his travels.

The idea of a separation from Meta was almost more than he could endure. "What will she think," said he, "of this sudden disappearance, when she no longer meets me in her way to church? Will she not think me perfidious, and banish me from her heart?" Such ideas as these caused him infinite pain; and for a long while he could not devise any means of acquainting Meta with his plans; but at length the fertile genius of love furnished him with the following idea :—Francis went to the curate, of the church which his mistress daily frequented, and requested him before the sermon and during mass to put up prayers for *a happy issue to the affairs of a young traveller;* and these prayers were to be continued till the moment of his return, when they were to be changed into those of thanks.

Every thing being arranged for his departure, he mounted his steed, and passed close under Meta's window. He saluted her with a very significant air, and with much less caution than heretofore. The young girl blushed deeply; and mother Bridget took this opportunity of loudly expressing her dislike to this bold adventurer, whose impertinence and foppery induced him to form designs on her daughter.

From this period the eyes of Meta in vain searched for Francis. She constantly heard the prayer which was put up for him; but was so en-

tirely absorbed by grief at no longer perceiving the
object of her affection,.that she paid no attention
to the words of the priest. In no way could she
account for his disappearing. Some months afterwards, her grief being somewhat ameliorated, and
her mind more tranquillized, when she was one day
thinking of the last time she had seen Francis, the
prayer arrested her attention ; she reflected for an
instant, and quickly divined for whom it was said ;
she naturally joined in it with great fervour, and
strongly recommended the young traveller to the
protection of her guardian angel.

Meanwhile Francis continued his journey, and
had travelled the whole of a very sultry day over
one of the desert cantons of Westphalia without
meeting with a single house. As night approached,
a violent storm came on : the rain fell in torrents;
and poor Francis was soaked to the very skin. In
this miserable situation he anxiously looked around,
and fortunately discovered in the distance a light,
towards which he directed his horse's steps; but
as he drew near, he beheld a miserable cottage,
which did not promise him much succour, for it
more resembled a stable than the habitation of a
human being. The unfeeling wretch who inha-
bited it refused him fire or water as if he had been
a banished man—he was just about to extend
himself on the straw in the midst of the cattle, and

his indolence prevented his lighting a fire for the
stranger. Francis vainly, endeavoured to move
the peasant to pity: the latter was inexorable, and
blew out his candle with the greatest *nonchalance*
possible, without bestowing a thought on Francis.
However, as the traveller hindered him from sleeping, by his incessant lamentations and prayers, he
was anxious to get rid of him.

"Friend," said he to him, "if you wish to be
accommodated, I promise you it will not be here;
but ride through the little wood to your left-hand,
and you will find the castle belonging to the chevalier Eberhard Bronkhorst, who is very hospitable
to travellers; but he has a singular mania, which
is, to flagellate all whom he entertains: therefore
decide accordingly."

Francis, after considering for some minutes
what he had best do, resolved on hazarding the adventure. "In good faith," said he, "there is no
great difference between having one's back broken
by the miserable accommodation of a peasant, or
by the chevalier Bronkhorst: friction disperses fever; possibly its effects may prove beneficial to me,
if I am compelled to keep on my wet garments."

Accordingly he put spurs to his horse, and very
shortly found himself before a gothic castle, at the
iron gate of which he loudly knocked: and was
answered from within by " *Who's there?*" But

ere he was allowed time to reply, the gate was
opened. However, in the first court he was compelled to wait with patience, till they could learn
whether it was the lord of the castle's pleasure to
flagellate a traveller, or send him out to pass the
night under the canopy of heaven.

This lord of the castle had from his earliest infancy served in the Imperial army, under command
of George of Frunsberg, and had himself led a
company of infantry against the Venetians. At
length, however, fatigued with warfare, he had retired to his own territory, where, in order to ex-
piate the crimes he had committed during the several campaigns he had been in, he did all the
good and charitable acts in his power. But his
manner still preserved all the roughness of his former profession. The newly arrived guest, although disposed to submit to the usages of the
house for the sake of the good fare, could not help
feeling a certain trembling of fear as he heard the
bolts grating, ere the doors were opened to him;
and the very doors by their groaning noise seemed
to presage the catastrophe which awaited him. A
cold perspiration came over him as he passed the
last door; but finding that he received the utmost
attention, his fears a little abated. The servants
assisted him in getting off his horse, and unfastened
his cloak-bag; some of them led his horse to the

stable, while others preceding him with flambeaux conducted Francis to their master, who awaited his arrival in a room magnificently lighted up.

Poor Francis was seized with an universal tremour, when he beheld the martial air and athletic form of the lord, of the castle, who came up to him and shook him by the hand with so much force that he could scarcely refrain from crying out, and in a thundering voice enough to stun him, told him "he was welcome." Francis shook like an aspen-leaf in every part of his body.

"What ails you, my young comrade?" cried the chevalier Bronkhorst, in his voice of thunder: "What makes you thus tremble, and renders you as pale as if death had actually seized you by the throat?"

Francis recovered himself; and knowing that his shoulders would pay the reckoning, his fears gave place to a species of audacity.

"My lord," answered he with confidence, "you see that I am so soaked with rain that one might suppose I had swam through the Wezer; order me therefore some dry clothes instead of those I have on, and let us then drink a cup of hot wine, that I may, if possible, prevent the fever which otherwise may probably seize me. It will comfort my heart."

"Admirable!" replied the chevalier; "ask for

whatever you want, and consider yourself here as
at home."

Accordingly Francis gave his orders like a baron of high degree: he sent away the wet clothes,
made choice of others, and, in fine, made himself
quite at his ease. The chevalier, so far from expressing any dissatisfaction at his free and easy
manners, commanded his people to execute whatever he ordered with promptitude, and condemned
some of them as blockheads who did not appear to
know how to wait on a stranger. As soon as the table
was spread, the chevalier seated himself at it with
his guest : they drank a cup of hot wine together.

" Do you wish for any thing to eat ?" demanded
the lord of Francis.

The latter desired he would order up what his
house afforded, that he might see whether his
kitchen was good.

No sooner had he said this, than the steward
made his appearance, and soon furnished up a
most delicious repast. Francis did not wait for his
being requested to partake of it : but after having
made a hearty meal, he said to the lord of the
castle, " Your kitchen is by no means despicable;
if your cellar is correspondent, I cannot but say
you treat your guests nobly."

The chevalier made a sign to his butler, who
brought up some inferior wine, and filled a large

glass of it to his master, who drank to his guest. Francis instantly returned the compliment.

"Well, young man, what say you to my wine?" asked the chevalier.

"'Faith," replied Francis, "I say it is bad, if it is the best you have in your cellar; but if you have none worse, I do not condemn it."

"You are a connoisseur;" answered the chevalier. "Butler, bring us a flask of older wine."

His orders being instantly attended to, Francis tasted it. "This is indeed some good old wine, and we will stick to it if you please."

The servants brought in a great pitcher of it; and the chevalier, being in high good-humour, drank freely with his guest; and then launched out into a long history of his several feats of prowess in the war against the Venetians. He became so overheated by the recital, that in his enthusiasm he overturned the bottles and glasses, and flourishing his knife as if it were a sword, passed it so near the nose and ears of Francis, that he dreaded he should lose them in the action.

Though the night wore away, the chevalier did not manifest any desire to sleep; for he was quite in his element, whenever he got on the topic of the Venetian war. Each succeeding glass added to the heat of his imagination as he proceeded in his narration, till at length Francis began to apprehend

that it was the prologue to the tragedy in which
he was to play the principal part; and feeling
anxious to learn whether he was to pass the night
in the castle, or to be turned out, he asked for a
last glass of wine to enable him to sleep well. He
feared that they would commence by filling him
with wine, and that if he did not consent to continue drinking, a pretext would be laid hold of for
driving him out of the castle with the usual chastisement.

However, contrary to his expectation, the lord
of the castle broke the thread of his narration, and
said to him : " Good friend, every thing in its
place : to-morrow we will resume our discourse."

" Excuse me, sir knight," replied Francis ; " to-
morrow, before sun-rise, I shall be on my road.
The distance from hence to Brabant is very considerable, and I cannot tarry here longer, therefore permit me to take leave of you now, that I
may not disturb you in the morning."

" Just as you please about that : but you will
not leave the castle before I am up ; we will breakfast together, and I shall accompany you to the
outer gate, and take leave of you according to my
usual custom."

Francis needed no comment to render these
words intelligible. Most willingly would he have
dispensed with the chevalier's company to the gate;

but the latter did not appear at all inclined to de-
viate from his usual custom.; He ordered his servants to assist the stranger in undressing, and to
take care of him till he was in bed. · · ..

Francis found his bed an excellent one; and ere
he went to sleep, he owned that so handsome a reception was not dearly bought at the expense of a
trifling beating. The most delightful dreams (in
which Meta bore the sway) occupied him the
whole night; and he would have gone on (thus
dreaming) till mid-day, if the sonorous voice of the
chevalier and the clanking of his spurs had not
disturbed him. :

It needed all Francis's efforts to quit this delightful bed, in which he was so comfortable, and
where he knew himself to be in safety: he turned
from side to side; but the chevalier's tremendous
voice was like a death-stroke to him, and at
length he resolved to get up. Several servants assisted him in dressing; and the chevalier waited for
him at a small but well-served table; but Francis,
knowing the moment of trial was at hand, had no
great inclination to feast. The chevalier tried to
persuade him to eat, telling him it was the best
thing to keep out the fog and damp air of the
morning.

" Sir knight," replied Francis, " my stomach is
still loaded from your excellent supper of last

P

evening; but my pockets are empty, and I should much like to fill them, in order to provide against future wants." . . . .

The chevalier evinced his pleasure at his frankness by filling his pockets with as much as they could contain. As soon as they brought him his horse, which he discovered had been well groomed and fed, he drank the last glass of wine to say Adieu, expecting that at that signal the chevalier would take him by the collar and make him pay his welcome. But, to his no small surprise, the chevalier contented himself with heartily shaking him by the hand as on his arrival : and as soon as the gate was opened, Francis rode off safe and sound. . . . .

In no way could our traveller account for his host permitting him thus to depart without paying the usual score. At length he began to imagine that the peasant had simply told him the story to frighten him ; and feeling a curiosity to learn whether or not it had any foundation in fact, he rode back to the castle. The chevalier had not yet quitted the gate, and was conversing with his servants on the pace of Francis's horse, who appeared to trot very roughly : and seeing the traveller return, he supposed that he had forgotten something, and by his looks seemed to accuse his servants of negligence.

"What do you want, young man?" demanded
he: "Why do you, who were so much pressed for
time, return?" ... ill... i ....)
"Allow me, most noble sir," replied Francis,
"to ask you one question; for there are reports
abroad which tend to vilify you: It is said, that,
after having hospitably received and entertained
strangers, you make them at their departure feel
the weight of your arm. And although I gave credence to this rumour, I have omitted nothing which
might have entitled me to this mark of your favour.
But, strange to say, you have permitted me to depart in peace, without even the slightest mark of
your strength. You see my surprise; therefore do
pray inform me whether there is any foundation for
the report, or whether I shall chastise the impu-
dent story-teller who related the false tale to me."

"Young man," replied Bronkhorst, "you have
heard nothing but the truth: but it needs some
explanations.——I open my door hospitably to
every stranger, and in Christian charity I give them
a place at my table; but I am a man who hates
form or disguise; I say all I think, and only wish
in return that my guests openly and undisguisedly
ask for all they want. There are unfortunately,
however, a tribe of people who fatigue by their
mean complaisance and ceremonies without end;
who wear me out by their dissimulation, and stun

me by propositions devoid of sense, or who do not
conduct themselves with decency during the repast.
Gracious heavens ! I lose all patience when they
carry their fooleries to such excesses, and I exert
my right as master of the castle, by taking hold of
their collars, and giving them tolerably severe chastisement ere I turn them out of my gates.—But a
man of your sort, my young friend, will ever be
welcome under my roof; for you boldly and openly
ask for what you require, and say what you think;
and such are the persons I admire. If in your way
back you pass through this canton, promise me
you will pay me another visit. Good bye ! Let
me caution you never to place implicit confidence
in any thing you hear; believe only that there may
be a single grain of truth in the whole story : be
always frank, and you will succeed through life.
Heaven's blessings attend you."

Francis continued his journey towards Anvers
most gaily, wishing, as he went, that he might every
where meet with as good a reception as at the chevalier Bronkhorst's.

Nothing remarkable occurred during the rest of
his journey: and he entered the city full of the
most sanguine hopes and expectations. In every
street his fancied riches stared him in the face.
"It appears to me," said he, "that some of my
father's debtors must have succeeded in business,

and that they will only require my presence to re-
pay their debts with honour."

   After having rested from the fatigue of his journey, he made himself acquainted with every particular relative to the debtors, and learnt that the
greater part had become rich, and were doing extremely well. This intelligence reanimated his
hopes : he arranged his papers, and paid a visit to
each of the persons who owed him any thing. But
his success was by no means what he had expected : some of the debtors pretended that they had
paid every thing; others, that they had never heard
mention of Melchior of Bremen; and the rest produced accounts precisely contradictory to those he
had, and which tended to prove they were creditors
instead of debtors. In fine, ere three days had
elapsed, Francis found himself in the debtors-pri-
son, from whence he stood no chance of being released till he had paid the uttermost farthing of his
father's debts.

   How pitiable was this poor young man's condition! Even the horrors of the prison were augmented by the remembrance of Meta :—nay, to
such a pitch of desperation was he carried, that he
resolved to starve himself. Fortunately, however,
at twenty-seven years of age such determinations
are more easily formed than practised.

   The intention of those who put him into con-

finement was not merely with a view of exacting
payment of his pretended debts, but to avoid paying him his due : so, whether the prayers put up
for poor Francis at Bremen were effectual, or that
the pretended creditors were not disposed to maintain him during his life, I know not ; but after a
detention of three months they liberated Francis
from prison, with a particular injunction to quit the
territories of Anvers within four-and-twenty hours,
and never to set his foot within that city again :—
They gave him at the same time five florins to defray his expenses on the road. As one may well
imagine, his horse and baggage had been sold to
defray the costs incident to the proceedings.

With a heart overloaded with grief he quitted
Anvers, in a very different frame of mind to what
he experienced at entering it. Discouraged and ir-
resolute, he mechanically followed the road which
chance directed : he paid no attention to the various travellers, or indeed to any object on the road,
till hunger or thirst caused him to lift his eyes to
discover a steeple or some other token announcing
the habitation of human beings. In this state of
mind did he continue journeying on for several
days incessantly; nevertheless a secret instinct im-
pelled him to take the road leading to his own
country.

All on a sudden he roused as if from a profound

sleep, and recollected the place in which he was:
he stopped an instant to consider whether he should
continue the road he was then in, or return;
" For," said he, "what a shame to return to my
native city a beggar !" How could he thus return
to that city in which he formerly felt equal to the
richest of its inhabitants? How could he as a beggar present himself before Meta, without causing
her to blush for the choice she had made? He did
not allow time for his imagination to complete this
miserable picture, for he instantly turned back, as
if already he had found himself before the gates of
Bremen, followed by the shouts of the children.
His mind was soon made up as to what he should
do: he resolved to go to one of the ports of the
Low-Countries, there to engage himself as sailor
on board a Spanish vessel, to go to the newly discovered world; and not to return to his native
country till he had amassed as much wealth as he
had formerly so thoughtlessly squandered. In the
whole of this project, Meta was only thought of at
an immeasurable distance: but Francis contented
himself with connecting her in idea with his future
plans, and walked, or rather strode along, as if by
hurrying his pace he should sooner gain possession
of her.

Having thus attained the frontiers of the Low-
Countries, he arrived at sun-set in a village situ-

ated near Rheinburg ; but since entirely destroyed
in the thirty years' war. A caravan of carriers from
Liege filled the ·inn' so entirely, that the landlord
told Francis he could not give him 'a lodging; adding, that at the adjoining village he would find ac-
commodations.—Possibly he was actuated to this
refusal by Francis's appearance, who certainly in
point of garb might well· be mistaken for a vaga-
bond.

The landlord took him for a spy to a band of
thieves, sent probably to rob the carriers : so that
poor Francis, spite of his extreme lassitude,· was
compelled with his wallet at his back to proceed
on his road ; and having at his departure muttered
through his teeth some bitter maledictions against
the cruel· and ·unfeeling landlord, the latter appeared touched with compassion for the poor
stranger, and from the door of the inn called after
him: " Young man; a word with you! If you resolve on passing the night here, I will procure you
a lodging in that castle you now see on the hill;
there you will have rooms in abundance, provided
you are not afraid of being alone, for it is uninhabited. See, here are the keys belonging to it."

Francis joyfully accepted the landlord's proposition, and thanked him for it as if it had been an act
of great charity.

" It is to me a matter of little moment where I

pass the night, provided I am at my ease, and have
something to eat." But the landlord was an ill-
tempered fellow; and wishing to revenge the invec-
tives Francis had poured forth against him, he sent
him to the castle in order that he might be tormented by the spirits which were said to frequent it. :
: This castle was situated on a steep rock, and
was only separated from the village by the high-
road and a little rivulet.. Its delightful prospects
caused it to be kept in good repair, and to be well
furnished, as its owner made use of it as a hunt-
ing-seat : but no sooner did night come on than he
quitted it, in order to avoid the apparitions and
ghosts which haunted it; but during the day nothing
of the sort was visible, and all was tranquil.

When it was quite dark, Francis with a lantern
in his hand proceeded towards the castle. The
landlord accompanied him, and carried a little basket of provisions, to which he had added a bottle of
wine (which he said would stand the test), as well
as two candles and two wax-tapers for the night.
Francis, not thinking he should require so many
things, and being apprehensive he should have to
pay for them, asked why they were all brought.

" The light from my lantern," said he, " will
suffice me till the time of my getting into bed ;
and ere I shall get out of it, the sun will have risen,
for I am quite worn out with fatigue."

"I will not endeavour to conceal from you," replied the landlord, "that according to the current reports this castle is haunted by evil spirits; but do not let that frighten you; you see I live sufficiently near, that, in case any thing extraordinary should happen to you, I can hear you call, and shall be in readiness with my people to render you any assistance. At my house there is somebody stirring all night, and there is also some one constantly on the watch. I have lived on this spot for thirty years, and cannot say that I have ever seen any thing to alarm me: indeed, I believe that you may with safety attribute any noises you hear during the night in this castle, to cats and weazels, with which the granaries are overrun. I have only provided you with the means of keeping up a light in case of need, for, at best, night is but a gloomy season; and, in addition, these candles are consecrated, and their light will undoubtedly keep off any evil spirits, should there be such in the castle."

The landlord spoke only the truth, when he said he had not seen any ghosts in the castle; for he never had the courage to set his foot within its doors after dark; and though he now spoke so courageously, the rogue would not have ventured on any account to enter. After having opened the door, he gave the basket into Francis's hand, pointed out the way he was to turn, and wished

him good night: while the latter, fully satisfied
that the story of the ghosts must be fabulous, gaily
entered. He recollected all that had been told him
to the prejudice of the chevalier Bronkhorst, but
unfortunately forgot what that brave Castellan had
recommended to him at parting.

Conformably to the landlord's instructions, he
went up stairs and came to a door, which the key
in his possession soon unlocked: it opened into a
long dark gallery, where his very steps re-echoed;
this gallery led to a large hall, from which issued
a suite of apartments furnished in a costly manner:
he surveyed them all; and made choice of one in
which to pass the night, that appeared rather more
lively than the rest. The windows looked to the
high-road, and every thing that passed in front of
the inn could be distinctly heard from them. He
lighted two candles, spread the cloth, ate very
heartily, and felt completely at his ease so long as
he was thus employed; for while eating, no
thought or apprehension of spirits molested him;
but he no sooner arose from table, than he began
to feel a sensation strongly resembling fear.

In order to render himself secure, he locked the
door, drew the bolts, and looked out from each
window; but nothing was to be seen. Every thing
along the high-road and in front of the inn was
tranquil; where, contrary to the landlord's asser-

tions, not a single light was discernible. The sound
of the horn belonging to the night-guard was the
only thing that interrupted the silence which uni-
versally prevailed.

Francis closed the windows, once again looked
round the room, and after snuffing the candles that
they might burn the better, he threw himself on
the bed, which he found good and comfortable :
but although greatly fatigued, he could not get to
sleep so soon as he had hoped. A slight palpita-
tion of the heart, which he attributed to the agitation produced by the heat of his journey, kept him
awake for a considerable time, till at length sleep
came to his aid. After having as he imagined
been asleep somewhat about an hour, he awoke
and started up in a state of horror possibly not un-
usual to a person, whose blood is overheated :
this idea in some degree allayed his apprehensions;
and he listened attentively, but could hear nothing
excepting the clock, which struck the hour of midnight. Again he listened for an instant; and turning on his side, he was just going off to sleep again,
when he fancied he heard a distant door grinding
on its hinges, and then shut with a heavy noise.
In an instant the idea of the ghost approaching
caused him no little fear: but he speedily got the
better of his alarm, by fancying it was only the
wind; however, he could not comfort himself long

with this idea, for the sound approached nearer and
nearer, and resembled the noise made by the
clanking of chains, or the rattling of a large bunch
of keys.

The terror which Francis experienced was beyond all description, and he put his head under the
clothes. The doors continued to open with a
frightful noise, and at last he heard some one try-
ing different keys at the door of his room; one of
them seemed perfectly to fit the lock, but the bolts
kept the door fast; however, a violent shock like a
clap of thunder caused them to give way, and in
stalked a tall thin figure with a black beard, whose
appearance was indicative of chagrin and melancholy. He was habited in the antique style, and on
his left shoulder wore a red cloak or mantle, while
his head was covered with a high-crowned hat.
Three times with slow and measured steps he
walked round the room, examined the consecrated
candles, and snuffed them: he then threw off his
cloak, unfolded a shaving apparatus, and took from
it the razors, which he sharpened on a large leather
strop hanging to his belt.

No powers are adequate to describe the agonies
Francis endured: he recommended himself to the
Virgin Mary, and endeavoured, as well as his fears
would permit, to form an idea of the spectre's designs on him. Whether he purposed to cut his

throat, or only take off his beard, he was at a loss
to determine. The poor traveller, however, was a
little more composed, when he saw the spectre
take out a silver shaving-pot, and in a bason of the
same metal put some water ; after which he made
a lather, and then placed a chair. But a cold perspiration came over Francis, when the spectre with
a grave air, made signs for him to sit in that chair.
He knew it was useless to resist this mandate,
which was but too plainly given: and thinking it
most prudent to make a virtue of necessity, and to
put a good face on the matter, Francis obeyed the
order, jumped nimbly out of bed, and seated himself as directed.

The spirit placed the shaving-bib round his
neck : then taking a comb and scissars, cut off his
hair and whiskers ; after which he lathered, according to rule, his beard, his eye-brows and head, and
shaved them all off, completely from his chin to
the nape of his neck. This operation ended, he
washed his head, wiped and dried it very nicely,
made him a low bow, folded up his case, put his
cloak on his shoulder, and made towards the door
to go away.

The consecrated candles had burnt most bril-
liantly during the whole of this operation; and by
their clear light Francis discovered, on looking into
the glass, that he had not a single hair remaining

on his head. Most bitterly did he deplore the loss
of his beautiful brown hair: but he regained courage on remarking, that, however great the sacrifice,
all was now over, and that the spirit had no more
power over him.

In effect, the ghost walked towards the door
with as grave an air as he had entered; but after
going a few steps, he stopped, looked at Francis
with a mournful air, and stroked his beard. He
three times repeated this action; and was on the
point of quitting the room, when Francis began to
fancy he wanted something. With great quickness
of thought he imagined it might be, that he wished
him to perform a like service for him to that which
he had just been executing on himself.

As the spectre, spite of his woe-begone aspect,
appeared more inclined to raillery than gravity; and
as his proceedings towards Francis appeared more
a species of frolic than absolute ill treatment, the
latter no longer appeared to entertain any apprehension of him; and in consequence determined
to hazard the adventure. He therefore beckoned
the phantom to seat himself in the chair. It instantly returned, and obeyed: taking off its cloak,
and unfolding the case, it placed it on the table,
and seated itself in the chair, in the attitude of one
about to be shaved. Francis imitated precisely all
he had seen it do: he cut off its hair and whis-

kers, and then lathered its head. The spirit did not move an inch. Our barber's apprentice did not handle the razor very dexterously; so that having taken hold of the ghost's beard against the grain, the latter made a horrible grimace. Francis did not feel much assured by this action: however, he got through the job as well as he could, and rendered the ghost's head as completely bald as his own.

Hitherto the scene between the two performers had passed in profound silence; but on a sudden the silence was interrupted by the ghost exclaiming with a smiling countenance :—" Stranger, I heartily thank you for the eminent service you have rendered me; for to you am I indebted for deliverance from my long captivity. During the space of three hundred years I have been immersed within these walls, and my soul has been condemned to submit to this chastisement as a punishment for my crimes, until some living being had the courage to exercise retaliation on me, by doing to me what I have done by others during my life.

" Count Hartmann formerly resided in this castle: he was a man who recognized no law nor superior; was of an arrogant and overbearing disposition; committed every species of wickedness, and violated the most sacred rights of hospitality : he played all sorts of malicious tricks to strangers

who sought refuge under his roof, and to the poor
who solicited his charity. I was his barber, and
did every thing to please him. No sooner did I
perceive a pious pilgrim; than in an endearing tone
I urged him to come into the castle, and prepared
a bath for 'him; and while he) was enjoying the
idea of being taken care of, I shaved his beard and
head quite close, and then turned him out of the
bye door, with raillery and ridicule. All this, was
seen by count Hartmann from his window, with a
sort of devilish pleasure, while the children would
assemble round the abused stranger, and pursue
him with cries of derision.

": " One day there came a holy man from a far
distant country ; he wore a penitentiary cross at his
back, and his devotion had imprinted scars on his
feet, hands, and sides ; his head was shaved, excepting a circle of hair left to resemble the crown
of thorns worn by our Saviour. He asked some
water to wash his feet as he passed by, and some
bread to eat. I instantly put him into the bath ;
but did not respect even *his* venerable head. Upon which the pilgrim pronounced this terrible
curse on me: ' Depraved wretch,' said he, ' know
that at your death, the formidable gates of heaven,
of hell, and of purgatory will alike be closed
against your sinful soul, which shall wander
through this castle, in the form of a ghost, until

Q

some nian, without being invited or constrained,
shall do to you, what you have so long done to
others."

" From that moment the marrow in my bones
dried up, and I became a perfect shadow; my
soul quitted my emaciated body, and remained
wandering within these walls, according to the prediction of the holy man. In vain did I look and
hope for release from the painful ties which held
me to earth; for know, that no sooner is the soul
separated from the body, than it aspires to the
blissful regions of peace, and the ardour of its
wishes causes years to appear as long as centuries,
while it languishes in a strange element. As a
punishment, I am compelled to continue the trade
that I had exercised during my life; but, alas! my
nocturnal appearance soon rendered this castle de-
serted. Now and then a poor pilgrim entered to
pass the night here: when they did, however, I
treated them all as I have done you; but not one
has understood me, or rendered me the only service which could deliver my soul from this sad ser-
vitude. Henceforth no spirit will haunt this castle;
for I shall now enjoy that repose of which I have
been so long in search. Once again let me thank
you, gallant youth; and believe, that had I power
over the hidden treasures of the globe, I would
give them all to you; but, unfortunately, during

my life riches did not fall to my lot, and this castle contains no store: however, listen to the advice I am now about to give you.

"Remain here till your hair has grown again; then return to your own country; and at that period of the year when the days and nights are of equal length, go on the bridge which crosses the Weser, and there remain till a friend, whom you will there meet, shall tell you what you ought to do to get possession of terrestrial wealth. When you are rolling in riches and prosperity, remember me; and on every anniversary of the day on which you released me from the heavy maledictions which overwhelmed me, cause a mass to be said for the repose of my soul. Adieu! I must now leave you."

Thus saying, the phantom vanished, and left his liberator perfectly astonished at the strange history he had just related. For a considerable time Francis remained immoveable, and reasoned with himself as to the reality of what he had seen; for he could not help fancying still that it was only a dream: but his closely shaved head soon convinced him that the event had actually taken place. He got into bed again, and slept soundly till mid-day. The malicious inn-keeper had been on the watch from dawn of day for the appearance of the traveller, in order that he might enjoy a laugh

Q 2

at his expense, and express his surprise at the
night's adventure. But after waiting till his patience was nearly exhausted, and finding it approached to noon, he began to apprehend that the
spirit had either strangled the stranger, or that he
had died of fright. He therefore called his servants together, and ran with them to the castle,
passing through every room till he reached the one
in which he had observed the light the over-night:
there he found a strange key in the door, which
was still bolted ; for Francis had drawn the bolts
again after the ghost had vanished. The landlord,
who was all anxiety, knocked loudly ; and Francis
on awaking, at first thought it was the phantom
come to pay him a second visit ; but at length recognising the landlord's voice, he got up and opened
the door. : : ' : :!!'

The landlord, affecting the utmost possible astonishment, clasped his hands together, and exclaimed, " Great God and all the saints ! then the *red*
cloak has actually been here and shaved you completely ? I now see that the story was but too
well founded. But pray relate to me all the particulars : tell me what the spirit was like ; how he
came thus to shave you ; and what he said to you ?"

Francis, having sense enough to discover his
roguery, answered him by saying : " The spirit resembled a man wearing a red cloak ; you know

full well how he performed the operation: and his conversation I perfectly remember;—listen attentively:—'Stranger,' said he to me, 'do not trust to a certain inn-keeper who has a figure of malice for his sign; the rogue knew well what would happen to you. Adieu! I now quit this abode, as my time is come; and in future no spirit will make its appearance here. I am now about to be transformed into a night-mare, and shall constantly torment and haunt this said inn-keeper, unless he does penance for his villany, by lodging, feeding, and furnishing you with every thing needful, till your hair shall grow again and fall in ringlets over your shoulders.'"

At these words the landlord was seized with a violent trembling: he crossed himself, and vowed to the Virgin Mary that he would take care of the young stranger, lodge him, and give him every thing he required free of cost. He then conducted him to his house, and faithfully fulfilled what he promised.

The spirit being no longer heard or seen, Francis was naturally looked on as a conjuror. He several times passed a night in the castle; and one evening a courageous villager accompanied him, and returned without having lost his hair. The lord of the castle, hearing that the formidable *red cloak* was no longer to be seen, was quite delighted,

and gave orders that the stranger who had delivered
him from this spirit should be well taken care of.
. Early in the month of September, Francis's hair
began to form into ringlets, and he prepared to
depart; for all his thoughts were directed towards
the bridge over the Weser, where he hoped, according to the barber's predictions, to find the friend
who would point out to him the way to make his
fortune.

. When Francis took leave of the landlord, the
latter presented him with a handsome horse well
appointed, and loaded with a large cloak-bag on
the back of the saddle, and gave him at the same
time a sufficient sum of money to complete his
journey. This was a present from the lord of the
castle, expressive of his thanks for having delivered
him from the spirit, and rendered his castle again
habitable.

Francis arrived at his native place in high spirits. He returned to his lodging in the little street,
where he lived very retired, contenting himself for
the present with secret information respecting Meta.
All the tidings he thus gained were of a satisfactory nature; but he would neither visit her, nor
make her acquainted with his return, till his fate
was decided.

He waited with the utmost impatience for the
equinox ; till which, time seemed immeasurably

long. The night preceding the eventful day, he
could not close his eyes to sleep ; and that he
might be sure of not missing the friend with whom
as yet he was unacquainted, he took his station ere
sun-rise on the bridge, where no human being but
himself was to be discovered. Replete with hopes
of future good fortune, he formed a thousand projects in what way to spend his money. : :

Already had he, during the space of nearly an
hour, traversed the bridge alone, giving full scope to
his imagination ; when on a sudden the bridge presented a moving scene, and amongst others, many
beggars took their several stations on it, to levy
contributions on the passengers. The first of this
tribe who asked charity of Francis was a poor devil with a wooden leg, who, being a pretty good
physiognomist, judged from the gay and contented
air of the young man that his request would be
crowned with success; and his conjecture was not
erroneous, for he threw a demi-florin into his hat.

Francis, meanwhile, feeling persuaded that the
friend he expected must belong to the highest class
of society, was not surprised at not seeing him at
so early an hour, and waited therefore with patience. But as the hour for visiting the Exchange
and the Courts of Justice drew near, his eyes were
in constant motion. He discovered at an immense
distance every well-dressed person who came on

the bridge, and his blood was in a perfect ferment
as each approached him, for in some one of them,
did he hope to discover the author of his good fortune; but it was in vain his looking the people in.
the face, no one paid attention to him. .The beggars, who at noon were seated on the ground eating their dinner, remarking that the young man
they had seen from the first of the morning was'
the only person remaining with them on the bridge,
and that he had not spoken to any one, or appeared
to have any employment, took him for a lazy va-
gabond; and although they had received marks of
his beneficence, they began to make game of him,
and in derision called him the *provost* of the bridge.
The physiognomist with the wooden leg remarked
that his air was no longer so gay as in the morning,
and that having drawn his hat over his face he appeared entirely lost in thought, for he walked
slowly along, nibbling an apple with an abstracted
air. The observer, resolving to benefit by what he
had remarked, went to the further extremity of the
bridge, and after well examining the visionary, came
up to him as a stranger, asked his charity, and succeeded to his utmost wish; for Francis, without
turning round his head, gave him another demi-
florin.

· In the afternoon a crowd of new faces presented.
themselves to Francis's observation, while he be-

came quite weary at his friend's tardiness; but hope
still kept up his attention. ·-However, the fast declining sun gave notice of the approach of night, and
yet scarcely any of the many passers-by had noticed
Francis. Some few, perhaps, had returned his salutation, but not one had, as he expected and
hoped, embraced him. At length, the day so visibly declined that the bridge became nearly de-
serted; for even the beggars went away. A profound melancholy seized the heart of poor Francis,
when he found his hopes thus deceived; and giving way to despair, he would have precipitated
himself into the Weser, had not the recollection of
Meta deterred him. He felt anxious, ere he terminated his days in so tragical a manner, to see her
once again as she went to mass, and feast on the
contemplation of her features.

He was preparing to quit the bridge, when the
beggar with the wooden leg accosted him, for he
had in vain puzzled his brains to discover what
could possibly have caused the young man to remain on the bridge from morning till night. The
poor cripple had waited longer than usual on account of Francis, in order to see when he went;
but as he remained longer than he wished, curiosity at length induced him openly to address him,
in order to learn what he so ardently desired to
know.

"Pray excuse me, worthy sir," said he; "and permit me to ask you a question."

Francis, who was by no means in a mood to talk, and who now heard from the mouth of a beggar the words which he had so anxiously expected from a friend, answered him in rather an angry tone: "Well then! what is it you want to know, old man?"

"Sir, you and I were the two first persons on this bridge to-day; and here we are still the only remaining two. As for me and my companions, it is pretty clear that we only come to ask alms: but it is equally evident you do not belong to our profession; and yet you have not quitted the bridge the whole day. My dear sir, for the love of God, if it is no secret, tell me I entreat you for what purpose you came, and what is the grief that rends your heart?"

"What can it concern you, old dotard, to know where the shoe pinches me, or what afflictions I am labouring under?"

"My good sir, I wish you well; you have twice bestowed your charity on me, which I hope the Almighty will return to you with interest. I could not but observe, however, that this evening your countenance no longer looked gay and happy as in the morning; and, believe me, I was sorry to see the change."

The unaffected interest evinced by the old man pleased Francis. " Well," replied he, " since you attach so much importance to the knowledge of the reason I have for remaining the whole day here plaguing myself, I will inform you that I came in search of a friend who appointed to meet me on this bridge, but whom I have expected in vain."

" With your permission I should say your friend is a rogue, to play the fool with you in this manner. If he had so served me, I should make him feel the weight of my crutch whenever I met him: for if he has been prevented from keeping his word by any unforeseen obstacle, he ought at least to have sent to you, and not have kept you here on your feet a whole day."

" And yet I have no reason to complain of his not coming, for he promised me nothing. In fact, it was only in a dream that I was told I should meet a friend here."

Francis spoke of it as a dream, because the history of the ghost was too long to relate.

" That alters the case," replied the old man. " Since you rest your hopes on dreams, I am not astonished at your being deceived. I have also had many dreams in my life; but I was never fool enough to pay attention to them. If I had all the treasures that have been promised me in dreams, I could purchase the whole city of Bremen : but

I have never put faith in dreams, and have not
taken a single step to prove whether they were
true or false ; for I know full well, it would be
useless trouble : and I am astonished that you
should have lost so fine a day, which you might
have employed so much more usefully, merely on
the strength of a dream which appears to me so
wholly devoid of sense or meaning."

" The event proves the justness of your remark,
old father ; and that dreams generally are deceitful.
But it is rather more than three months since I had
a very circumstantial dream relative to my meeting
a friend on this particular day, here on this bridge;
and it was so clearly indicated that he should communicate things of the utmost importance, that I
thought it worth while to ascertain whether this
dream had any foundation in truth."

" Ah! sir, no one has had clearer dreams than
myself; and one of them I shall never forget. I
dreamt, several years since, that my good angel
stood at the foot of my bed, in the form of a young
man, and addressed me as follows :—' Berthold,
listen attentively to my words, and do not lose any
part of what I am about to say. A treasure is al-
lotted you; go and secure it, that you may be enabled to live happily the rest of your days. To-
morrow evening, when the sun is setting, take a
pick-axe and spade over your shoulder, and go out

of the city by the gate leading to Hamburgh: when
you arrive facing the convent of Saint Nicholas,
you will see a garden, the entrance to which is or-
namented by two pillars ; conceal yourself behind
one of these until the moon rises : then push the
door hard, and it will yield to your efforts ; go
without fear into the garden, follow a walk covered
by a treillage of vines, and to the left you will see a
great apple-tree: place yourself at the foot of this
tree, with your face turned towards the moon, and
you will perceive, at fifteen feet distance, two
bushy rose-trees: search between these two shrubs,
and at the depth of about six feet you will discover
a great flag-stone, which covers the treasure in-
closed within an iron chest ; and although it is
heavy and difficult to handle, do not regret the labour it will occasion you to move it from the hole
where it now is. You will be well rewarded for
your pains and trouble, if you look for the key
which is hid under the box.'"

Francis remained like one stupified at this recital; and certainly would have been unable to conceal his astonishment, if the darkness of the night
had not favoured him. The various particulars
pointed out by the beggar brought to his recollection a little garden which he had inherited from his
father, and which garden was the favourite spot of
that good man ; but possibly for that very reason

it was not held in estimation by the son. Melchior had caused it to be laid out according to his
own taste, and his son in the height of his extravagance had sold it at a very low price.

The beggar with his wooden leg was now become a very interesting personage to Francis, who
perceived that he was the friend alluded to by the
ghost in the castle of Rummelsbourg. The first
impulse of joy would have led him to embrace the
mendicant; but he restrained his feelings, thinking
it best not to communicate the result of his intelligence to him.

"Well, my good man," said he, "what did you
when you awoke? did you not attend to the advice
given by your good angel?"

"Why should I undertake a hopeless labour?
It was only a vague dream; and if my good angel
was anxious to appear to me, he might choose a
night when I am not sleeping, which occurs but
too frequently: but he has not troubled his head
much about me; for if he had, I should not have
been reduced, as I now am, to his shame, to beg
my bread."

Francis took from his pocket another piece of
money, and gave it to the old man, saying: "Take
this to procure half a pint of wine, and drink it ere
you retire to rest. Your conversation has dispelled
my sorrowful thoughts; do not fail to come regu-

larly to this bridge, where I hope we shall meet
again." : ...   ·   ·   .. . . . , *l.* :   :*·
     The old lame man, not having for a long while
made so good a day's work, overwhelmed Francis
with his grateful benedictions. They separated,
and each went their way. Francis, whose joy was
at its height from the near prospect of his hopes
being realised, very speedily reached his lodging in
the bye street. ·   ,   . . ·. .   :   · · ,. .. . \ !
     The following day he ran to the purchaser of
the little garden, and proposed. to re-purchase it;
The latter, to whom this property was of no particular value, and indeed who began to be tired of
it, willingly consented to part with it.   They very
soon agreed as to the conditions of the purchase,
and went immediately to sign the contract: with the
money he had found in his bag, as a gift from the
lord of Rummelsbourg, Francis paid down half the
price : he then procured the necessary tools for dig-
ging a hole in the earth, conveyed them to the garden,
waited till the moon was up, strictly adhered to the
instructions given him by the old beggar, set to
work, and without any unlucky adventure he obtained the hidden treasure. · · ·:. · . · · : · \ . :
     His father, as a precaution against necessity, had
buried this money, without any intention to deprive his son of this considerable portion of his
inheritance; but dying suddenly, he had carried

the secret to his grave, and nothing but a happy combination of circumstances could have restored this lost treasure to its rightful owner.

The chest filled with gold pieces was too heavy
for Francis to remove to his lodging without employing some person to assist him : and feeling unwilling to become a topic of general conversation,
he preferred concealing it in the summer-house
belonging to the garden, and fetching it at several
times. On the third day, the whole was safely conveyed to his lodging in the little back street.

Francis dressed himself in the best possible style,
and went to the church to request that the priest
would substitute for the prayers which had been
previously offered up, a thanksgiving *for the safe*
return of a traveller to his native country, after
having happily terminated his business. He concealed himself in a corner, where, unseen, he could
observe Meta. The sight of her gave him inex-
pressible delight, especially when he saw the beautiful blush which overspread her cheeks, and the
brilliancy of her eyes, when the priest offered up
the thanksgiving. A secret meeting took place as
had been formerly arranged; and so much was
Meta affected by it, that any indifferent person
might have divined the cause.

Francis repaired to the Exchange, set up again
in business, and in a very short time had enough to

·do; his fortune each succeeding day becoming bet- ·
ter known, his neighbours judged that he had had
greater luck than sense in his journey to collect his ·
father's debts. He hired a large house in the best
part of the town, engaged clerks, and continued his
business with laudable and indefatigable assiduity;
he conducted himself with the utmost propriety
and 'sagacity,' and abstained from the foolish extra-
vagancies which had formerly been his ruin.

·The re-establishment of Francis's fortune formed the general topic of conversation. Every one
was astonished at the success of his foreign voyage:
but in proportion to the spreading fame of his
riches, did Meta's tranquillity and happiness dimi-
nish ; for it appeared that her silent lover was now
in a condition to declare himself openly, and yet he
remained dumb, and only manifested his love by the
usual rencontre on coming out of church; and even
this species of rendezvous became less frequent,
which appeared to evince a diminution of his affection. :

·, Poor Meta's heart was now torn by jealousy;
for she imagined that the inconstant Francis was
offering up his vows to some other beauty. She
had experienced secret transports of delight on
learning the change of fortune of the man she
loved, not from interested motives and the wish to
participate in his bettered fortune herself, but

· R

from affection to her mother, who, since the failure
of the match with the rich brewer, absolutely
seemed to despair of ever enjoying happiness or
comfort in this world. When she thought Francis
faithless, she wished that the prayers put up for
him in the church had not been heard, and that his
journey had not been attended with such entire
success; for had he been reduced to means merely
sufficient to procure the necessaries of life, in all
probability he would have shared them with her.

Mother Bridget failed not to perceive her
daughter's uneasiness, and easily guessed the cause;
for she had heard of her old neighbour's surprising
return, and she knew he was now considered an
industrious intelligent merchant; therefore she
thought if his love for her daughter was what it
ought to be, he would not be thus tardy in declaring it; for she well knew Meta's sentiments towards him. However, feeling anxious to avoid the
probability of wounding her daughter's feelings,
she avoided mentioning the subject to her: but the
latter, no longer able to confine her grief to her
own bosom, disclosed it to her mother, and confided the whole to her.

Mother Bridget did not reproach her daughter
for her past conduct, but employed all her elo-
quence to console her, and entreated her to bear
up with courage under the loss of all her hopes :

-:" You must resign him," said she : " you scorned
at the happiness which presented itself to your ac-
ceptance, therefore you must now endeavour to be
resigned at its departure. ' Experience has taught
me that those hopes which appear the best founded
are frequently the most delusive; follow my example, and never again deliver up your heart. Do
not reckon on any amelioration of your condition, and you will be contented with your lot.
Honour this spinning-wheel which produces the
means of your subsistence, and then fortune and
riches will be immaterial to you: you may do
without them." / :. . . .i ı . . , i   ' .) ., ' · ;
. Thus saying, mother Bridget turned her wheel.
round with redoubled velocity, in order to make
up for the time lost in conversation. · She spoke
nothing but the truth to her daughter : for since
the opportunity was gone by when she hoped it
was possible to have regained her lost comforts,
she had in such a manner simplified her present
wants and projects of future life, that it was not in
the power of destiny to produce any considerable
derangement in them. . But as yet Meta was not
so great a philosopher; so that her mother's exhortations, consolations, and doctrines, produced a
precisely different effect on her from what they
were intended. Meta looked on herself as the de-:
stroyer of the flattering hopes her mother had en-

tertained. Although she did not formerly accept the offer of marriage proposed to her, and
even then could not have reckoned on possessing beyond the common necessaries of life; yet,
since she had heard the tidings of the great fortune
obtained by the man of her heart, her views had,
become enlarged, and she anticipated with pleasure,
that by her choice she might realize her mother's
wishes.

. Now, however, this golden dream had vanished:
Francis would not come again; and indeed they,
even began to talk in the city of an alliance about
to take place between him and a very rich young
lady of Anvers. This news was a death-blow
to poor Meta: she vowed she would banish him;
from her thoughts; but still moistened her work
with her tears.

. Contrary, however, to her vow, she was one day,
thinking of the faithless one: for whenever she
filled her spinning-wheel, she thought of the following distich, which her mother had frequently
repeated to her to encourage her in her work:

> " Spin the thread well; spin, spin it more,
> For see your intended is now at the door."

Some one did in reality knock gently at the door;
and mother Bridget went to see who it was.
Francis entered, attired as for the celebration of a

wedding.   Surprise for a while suspended mother
Bridget's faculties of speech. . Meta, blushing
deeply and trembling, arose from her seat, but was
equally unable with her mother to say a word.
Francis was the only one of the three who could
speak; and he candidly declared his love, and demanded of Bridget the hand of her daughter., The
good mother, ever attentive to forms, asked eight
days to consider the matter, although the tears of
joy which she shed, plainly evinced her ready and
prompt acquiescence: but Francis, all impatience,
would not hear of delay: finding which, she, conformable to her duty as a mother, and willing to satisfy Francis's ardour, adopted a mid-way, and left
the decision to her daughter. · The latter, obeying
the dictates of her heart, placed herself by the side
of the object of her tenderest affection; and Francis, transported with joy, thanked her by a kiss. ,·
·. The two lovers then entertained themselves with
talking over the delights of the time when they so
well communicated their. sentiments by signs,
Francis had great difficulty in tearing himself
away from Meta and such 'converse sweet,' but he
had an important duty to fulfil. ··
.· He directed his steps towards the bridge over
the Weser, where he hoped to find his old friend
with the wooden leg, whom he had by no means
forgotten, although he had delayed making the pro-

mised visit. The latter instantly recognised Francis; and no sooner saw him at the foot of the
bridge, than he came to meet him, and shewed
evident marks of pleasure at sight of him.

"Can you, my friend," said Francis to him, after returning his salutation, "come with me into
the new town and execute a commission? You
will be well rewarded for your trouble."

"Why not?—with my wooden leg I walk about
just as well as other people; and indeed have an
advantage over them, for it is never fatigued. I
beg you, however, my good sir, to have the kind-
ness to wait till the man with the grey great-coat
arrives."

"What has this man in the grey great-coat to do
with you?"

"He every day comes as evening approaches
and gives me a demi-florin; I know not from
whom. It is not indeed always proper to learn all
things; so I do not breathe a word. I am sometimes tempted to believe, that it is the devil who is
anxious to buy my soul; but it matters little, I
have not consented to the bargain, therefore it
cannot be valid."

"I verily believe that grey surtout has some malice in his head; so follow me, and you shall have
a quarter-florin over and above the bargain."

Francis conducted the old man to a distant cor-

ner, near the ramparts of the city, stopped before
a newly built house, and knocked at the door. As
soon as the door was opened, he thus addressed
the old beggar: " You have procured a very agreeable evening for me in the course of my life ; it is
but just, therefore, that I should shed some comforts over your declining days. This house and
every thing appertaining thereto belongs to you.
The kitchen and cellar are both well stocked ;
there is a person to take care of you, and every day
at dinner you will find a quarter-florin under your
plate. It is now time for you to know that the
man in the grey surtout is my servant, whom I
every day sent with my alms till this house was
ready to receive you. You may, if you please, consider me as your guardian angel, since your good
angel did not acquit himself uprightly in return for
your gratitude."

Saying this, he made the old man go into his
house; where the latter found every thing he could
possibly desire or want. The table was spread; and
the old man was so much astonished at this unexpected good fortune, that he thought it must be a
dream ; for he could in no way imagine why a
rich man should feel so much interest for a miserable beggar. Francis having again assured him
that every thing he saw was his own, a torrent of
tears expressed his thanks; and before he could suf-

·ficiently recover from his astonishment to express his gratitude by words, Francis had vanished.

The following day, mother Bridget's house was ·filled with merchants and shopkeepers of all de-·scriptions, whom Francis had sent to Meta, in or-der that she might purchase and get ready every ·thing she required for her appearance in the world with suitable *éclat.* Three weeks afterwards he conducted her to the altar. The splendour of the wedding far exceeded that of the *King of Hops.* Mother Bridget enjoyed the satisfaction of adorn-ing her daughter's forehead with the nuptial crown, and thereby obtained the accomplishment of all her desires, and was recompensed for her virtuous and active life. She witnessed her daughter's hap-piness with delight, and proved the very best of grand-mothers to her daughter's children.

THE END.

Printed by S. Hamilton, Weybridge.

Milton Keynes UK
Ingram Content Group UK Ltd.
UKHW021014180923
428892UK00005B/130